The   Piano

The Piano

A Novel
by

Jane Campion

and

Kate Pullinger

MIRAMAX BOOKS
HYPERION

New York

Book design by Margaret M. Wagner

Library of Congress Cataloging-in-Publication Data

Campion, Jane.
    The piano : the novel / by Jane Campion with Kate Pullinger. —
1st ed.

       p.   cm.
   ISBN 0-7868-8096-1
   1. Man-woman relationships—New Zealand—Fiction. 2. Mothers
and daughters—New Zealand—Fiction. 3. Married women—New
Zealand—Fiction. 4. Mute persons—New Zealand—Fiction.
5. Pianists—New Zealand—Fiction. I. Pullinger, Kate. II. Title.
PR9619.3.C345P53   1994
823—dc20   94-7325
                                           CIP

First Paperback Edition

10 9 8 7 6 5 4 3 2 1

Today I will not seek the shadowy region;

Its unsustaining vastness waxes drear;

And visions rising, legion after legion,

Bring the unreal world too strangely near.

EMILY BRONTE (1818–1848)

Prologue

THE story of Ada and her piano has been told and retold
by those in the small New Zealand settlement of
————, and by those back in Scotland who knew Ada
and her daughter, and her daughter's daughters. It was
not only women who spoke of the story; men talked
about it in public houses and fine houses, some shudder-
ing, others wondering at the lengths some would go for
love or passion. There was something irresistible in the
story that made it popular to all. Many liked to feign
horror, but could not contain their impatience if the
story were stopped, even for prayer. One woman claimed
to have heard and learnt the pieces Ada herself played
and had concerts of the piano music that could not accommodate all who wished to attend. Still, those who
went were disappointed as the story was not retold along
with the music, and some did not believe the music was
genuine.

Most of what was told was true in some points: that
Ada did not speak, that she had an illegitimate daughter,

and that she married a Scotsman whom she had never met and who had taken her, along with a small dowry, to the farthest country on the earth. But even these facts were not all true. Alisdair Stewart was already in New Zealand when Ada and her daughter traveled out to meet him. Almost all the stories fell apart, as most were told by observers who saw little of the entire episode. But Ada McGrath knew the whole story, and she told it to her daughter, Flora, when Flora herself was the mother of several children and Ada lay ill and dying in the small, pleasant town of Nelson. Ada was sixty-nine years old and happy she said.

What follows is a version of the story pieced together from the testimony of Flora herself and of others who knew the family, although the reader should be warned that the author of this strange tale has taken the liberty of embellishing these descriptions in the manner of all storytellers.

The voice you hear is not my speaking voice, but my mind's voice.

I have not spoken since I was six years old. No one knows why, not even me. My father says it is a dark talent and the day I take it into my head to stop breathing will be my last.

Today he married me to a man I've not yet met. Soon my daughter and I shall join him in his own country. My husband said my muteness does not bother him. He writes and hark this: God loves dumb creatures, so why not he!

Were good he had God's patience for silence affects everyone in the end. The strange thing is I don't think myself silent, that is, because of my piano. I shall miss it on the journey.

Chapter *1*

$\mathcal{B}$EYOND a desolate shore, on the edge of a far-off country, in a land of massy fern and flightless birds, a small surf-boat appeared, cutting through the swell and spray. Amidst the riotous sea, Ada McGrath and her daughter Flora were manhandled out of the boat and carried like human sacrifices on the shoulders of the seamen. Ada's voluminous black skirt spread across the men's arms and backs; she struggled to maintain some semblance of dignity, determined not to cry out. The seamen stumbled and braced themselves together against the chaotic waves; two were of African descent, all were battered, tattooed, and tough, some were drunk. Finally, Ada and Flora were set down on the empty black sand, unceremoniously. "Paddington Station," said one, but Ada did not smile or even hear, absorbed as she was in arrival. The sound of the sea breaking on the shore behind them was thunderous and huge.

Ada looked down at her boots, sinking into the wet and silvery sand, the sea rushing in around her, then up at the huge confusion of unfamiliar trees and creepers in the distance. Ada searched the cliffs—high and rugged and covered with the densest foliage she had ever seen—for some sign of life, fearful of it, yet full of curiosity at the same time. She was pale and dark and almost as diminutive as Flora, whose grave face and somber attire precisely mirrored her mother's. For the moment, Flora was bent on her knees, seasick as she had been almost every day of the voyage. Ada had never set eyes on a country like this, so unlike the stony coves and slow estuaries of Scotland. A green and thick screen of bush met the sky and the sea, and there was nothing, no people, no building, no track, no trace of the hand of man upon it. She had come to the end of the earth, it seemed, to meet a husband.

$\mathcal{A}$DA MCGRATH and her daughter Flora had journeyed for months across the rough ocean, night after night of being lulled, shifted, and harshly rocked in their ship beds, each day taking them farther and farther from Scotland. Sometimes Ada had lain awake at night, feeling the movement of the ship, and had wondered if she and Flora were traveling to Hell, or someplace darker. For this marriage by proxy, this wrenching away from home, felt to Ada like nothing less than a punishment for her sins.

On the journey Ada often dreamt of her husband Alisdair Stewart, whom she had not yet met, and her piano teacher, Delwar Haussler, whom she had not seen long since, and in her dreams the two men became one. In her dreams she was down in the cargo hold, playing the piano that was lashed in its box to the side of the ship like a beast that could not be allowed to escape. Music filled Ada's head, it calmed her, it enabled her to calm the child whose enthusiasm for the ship and its sailors shone brightly when she was not being sick in the old rusted bucket on the floor of their cabin. Conditions were bad, they had eaten no fresh food for weeks, only fish, dried and fresh, fried and boiled and baked, and Ada was sick of the taste of salt and scales.

From home shores they had enjoyed smooth sailing and the sensation of being adventure bound, yet once out of the Bay of Biscay they had sailed into a tremendous storm. The sea ran mountains high. Confined to their tiny cabin below deck, cramped even for people as small as Ada and Flora, they were thrown from floor to ceiling; for hours no news arrived, no knock at their door, their only communication from the ship itself as it groaned and was hammered by the sea. Ada was frightened then, more afraid than she had ever been, as they faced a peril more real and impassive than any concocted by polite society. But the old vessel was steadfast and had survived. Passengers emerged on deck to find that two sections of bulwark, a longboat, and one of the seamen had been washed overboard, but last rites were said and already the necessary repairs had been made. The sun shone on the calm azure sea, and it was as though waves had never raised and bucked their vessel, as if the storm had been but a nightmare induced by poor meals.

At home, Flora had kept a black Shetland pony named Gabriel, after the angel, and there had been her grandfather to spoil her. During their passage, Ada often wondered what this new life would hold for her daughter. The cargo held Ada's trousseau, though she did not think of it as such. She had slept each night with a small embroidered bag containing her dowry—jewelry, some gold, a banker's draft—under her pillow. Alisdair Stewart was waiting for them, but there were few other certainties. Ada told stories to Flora in their language of hand signs, but she had no real answers to Flora's continual questions about where this journey might end, so Flora invented her own: "We are going to meet a man, and he will kiss us awake, him a prince and we two princesses. And we will live together in a great palace and I shall do whatever I please." Ada did not speak, and Flora was her interpreter, but the child's stories had a life of their own.

Five months had passed and their journey was nearly complete. They had seen many things, touched the outermost perimeter of many lands; they had passed over the equator where the air was warm, and for weeks they had been in the company of flying fish, porpoises, and great seabirds. They had presently been traveling alongside land for some several hundred miles. Ada stared out from the deck of the ship. All she could see were dark cliffs, sometimes mountains behind; on many mornings the shore vanished, shrouded in mist. One afternoon, the ship slowed perceptibly, and the captain made it clear to Ada in his blustering way that this was where she and Flora were to disembark. A small craft was lowered over the side of the ship; it had been loaded with their possessions, all manner of boxes and cases, on top of which balanced the piano in its crate, which Ada's heart was pleased to see. Their progress hampered by their dresses and their tightly laced and slippery heeled leather boots, Ada and Flora climbed cautiously down the rope ladder, the ends of which trailed in the turquoise sea, and the boat took them toward the shimmering land.

*A*DA turned her face away from the impassive emerald forest and watched from a distance while the boxes and trunks were lifted out of the surfboat onto the beach. Several of the sailors were standing in a group, urinating openly, but Ada did not look their way. Her attention was diverted by the seamen who were now staggering through the waves with the piano. She stood on her toes and clenched her fists in anticipation and concern while it was precariously transported; she gestured urgently at the crew of filthy, tattered men until they brought it to higher, safer ground.

The strip of sand between the water and the cliffs was very wide with the low tide, a kind of broad halfway house between the steely sea and the verdant land. Ada stood on the beach, not yet arrived on the land, not yet departed from the ocean, feeling suddenly unable to turn to look at those cliffs again for fear their jade green face would make her feel unwelcome, a foreign visitor from too far away. The wind blew, strong and salty, and Ada could still feel the ship rocking beneath her feet. It would be many days before that sensation faded.

Ada ran toward her piano once it was placed on the beach and then, as though on a dock in a quay of a port, she inspected the instrument in its box, one hand in constant touch of it while her daughter gripped the other, keeping close by as though fearful of the sudden space she found herself in. The seamen talked, the wind bringing their words to her and then whipping the sound away again. There was no one to meet them. Perhaps this land contained no one at all.

"'Tis a dead shore, a dead shore," Ada heard a sailor say.

"Leave her alone, it's what we were told to do."

"A pox on you!"

"Aye, very nice, leave her and be lynched for the pleasure."

"Do what you like, I'm off this shore."

One of the older men, the leader of this small band, approached her. He wore a battered straw hat tied under his chin atop layers of waistcoats and jackets and woollen scarves that appeared to Ada to be all bound together by a layer of dirt. Behind him the other men kept their eyes out to sea or down on the sand; they did not want to be involved.

"It's a little rough out there. Could be they can't get

through to you in this weather. Maybe they'll come over land."

Ada nodded, the broad black ribbons of her bonnet flapping in the wind.

"Have you things for shelter?"

Ada signed to Flora, who interpreted her mother's hand gestures, speaking clearly and loudly: "She says 'Thank you.' "

The seaman made as though to walk back to his craft, then, suddenly uncertain that this was the right beach, turned and came back, concerned at the thought of leaving woman and child alone there. "Does your mother prefer to come on with us to Nelson?"

Ada signed vehemently to Flora, her expression one of cold dislike. She turned her back. "She says 'No,' " announced Flora, disgust creasing her small face. "She says she'd rather be boiled alive by natives than get back in your stinking tub."

The grizzled old seaman was sore aggrieved. He was accustomed to the gruesome banter of sailors, but not from the mouths of small girls and women. Ada, though she did not show it, enjoyed the license Flora took with her words, the child often voicing thoughts that an adult dare not speak aloud. The seaman took a step toward the girl. Ada quickly slipped in front of her child, frowning and protective. "You be damn fortuned I don't smack your puppy gob, missy!" the sailor said to Flora. "Damn lucky."

With that, the seamen left, pushing their boat out

across the sand until it was buoyant once again, leaving
Flora and Ada completely alone on the vast expanse of
the shore. The sun shone on the waves, playing every
shade of silver, gray and blue. Behind them a mist descended over the cliffs, which were hung with rainbows as
the light changed.

The slow hours passed. Flora helped Ada drag their
scattered belongings across the sand toward the piano;
the arrangement of crates and trunks and piano created
an odd semblance of a sitting room. Together they sat on
a packing crate, Ada clutching a dark red fringed umbrella to break the unceasing wind and, after a time, Flora
fell asleep.

The noise of the place astonished Ada, the seabirds
that circled overhead, the bush behind them where the
trees thrashed back and forth in the wind, the crash of the
waves where the sea met the land. Her eyes returned to
the cliffs again and again; the bush seemed so thick and
close, perhaps no one would appear. They would wait on
this beach forever, they could die here; Ada wondered for
a moment if her refusal of the seaman's offer had been
wise. But she quickly pushed her doubts to the back of
mind; after their journey she was prepared for any even-
tuality, nothing would cause her surprise. As Ada stroked
her daughter's face, she thought of that long journey, of
how its privations had hardened them both. Despite the
seasickness, and the homesickness—itself of a different
nature all together—Ada felt strong. She always felt
strong, a good constitution was one thing she did not

lack in her voiceless state. "You've a will like a stubborn mule, Ada McGrath," her maiden aunts used to say, disapprovingly. Ada was not sad to have left behind people such as her aunts; the only one that she would miss was her father. She did not allow herself to think of him now, so great was her longing. And yet it was he who had sent his daughter and grandchild away.

Still holding Flora's head on her lap, Ada pulled a fractured plank from the piano's crate where the wood had loosened. When she slipped her hand, with its new and still unfamiliar wedding band, between the slats, she was surprised to feel the coolness of the ivory keys beneath the tips of her fingers, a sensation of which she had been deprived for many months. She leaned forward, placed her head in its black bonnet on the box as if at prayer, and played a few notes. The sound soothed and reassured, but after a few moments the sweet familiarity and comfort of the piano seemed only to exaggerate the lonely uncertainty of that isolated place.

All at once a great rush of sea water shot straight under the raised crate of the piano, pushing the box out from where they sat, drenching their boots and the bottoms of their skirts with foam and brine and seaweed. Shaken from her reverie, Ada stood, aghast to discover that the tide had crept in completely unnoticed—while the rudely wakened Flora leapt shrieking onto the piano. They watched, helpless, as three of their boxes floated out to sea. Then, startled into movement, Ada waded out into the receding waves, rescuing the chicken cage, as one of the chickens was borne away on the tide, squawking. Ada began to run through the water toward the boxes that were floating farther and farther out to sea, but she stopped, feeling hopeless and dismayed, weighed down by her skirts as they grew heavy with the sea. Again, she turned and scanned the cliffs, but if there had been no one to greet them on arrival, there would surely be no one to rescue their belongings now.

Soon the sun began to go down, and Ada grew more concerned for their safety. In the gray-green light she ran with Flora along the broad ribbon of sand. The tide was now lowering once more, and the sand looked smooth and slippery like a seal's back. When they returned to their encampment, there was just a solitary pink streak left in the sky. Ada busied herself fashioning a makeshift tent, glad of the diversion the task gave her anxious mind. Composing a structure from her hooped crinoline cage covered with petticoats, and secured at the edges with stones, Ada was pleased by this good and practical use of garments unwieldy to wear; she was less certain of what they would be like to inhabit. Inside the tent she lit a candle, transforming the shelter into a giant, stranded Chinese lantern.

"Look. I'm a very great moth," Flora said, making shadow puppets with the light. "Will it catch fire?" she asked of their shelter, less fearful of the night outside than her mother. Ada made believe that all was well, their night on the beach a natural part of their journey. Cocooned inside, Ada told Flora a story to distract the child from awareness of their predicament, her hands motioning gracefully, sculpting the air, her face alight with expression, now tender, now sad, now humorous, now soft. "And the wind said, 'Remember how we used to play?' Then the wind took her hand and said, 'Come, come with me.' But she refused."

"Mumma, I have been thinking," Flora signed, then spoke with solemn expression. "I'm not going to call him Papa, I'm not going to call him anything. I'm not even going to look at him."

Presently Ada succeeded in quieting Flora, stroking her hair and face, and she was soon asleep. Ada herself lay awake, curled into the small space created by the hoops, and her thoughts swam backwards, into the past.

ADA MCGRATH of Aberdeen was six years old when her father felt unable to further delay an invitation to stay he had rashly made his two maiden aunts, Patricia and Ethel. They in turn campaigned to make it a rare family reunion, insisting that since they would be traveling such a distance it would be a prized opportunity to also see their unmarried cousin Gillian as well as her brother, wife, and boy. Ada's father, Wyston McGrath, finally agreed, thinking that the cousins might entertain each other. He had spent the last three weeks anxiously inventing urgent responsibilities that would take him from the house on to the estate for the best part of each day.

Wyston was a bad host, and as the appointed day approached his temper grew more difficult. Even small Ada (who had the talent to soothe any mood from him with her songs, sung with a passion odd in a child and a seriousness that beguiled not only Wyston but all the household) could do nothing for him. On occasion she would stroke and pat his hand with her tiny one, which he had always liked. But today these tender ministrations had no effect, as he irritably withdrew his hand to complain about the setting of the table being irksomely formal.

It was at length found that when one of the five candelabras was removed, it looked to McGrath's eyes correct. However, the next day he was unsure and, looking from one end of the room to the other, announced that four was a silly number and since the table was too long for three, it would have to be five.

The first day of the visit passed not well but satisfactorily in that the guests were well occupied looking all about the house, and the gamekeeper had, as instructed, exhausted the party with a long walk about the perimeter of the property. Ada was nervous of the visitors; she was too young to remember them from their last visit, so did not join them on their exploring but enjoyed very much watching them when they could not see her.

The incident, as it came to be known, happened on the third day of the visit at the long dinner table, now strangely bare of any candles. At the last moment McGrath had felt the issue best solved by removing them: "Now you see we have no problems with numbers."

Little Ada was seated between the two maiden aunts on a high chair especially made for her. The dinner was not going well. McGrath did not like the roast, pronouncing it tough and inedible. He insisted on it being sent back, but had not accounted for the fact that there was nothing else to replace it. The guests, whose plates had been taken from beneath them, were disappointed but stifled into making agreeably calming comments to their host and nephew. It was in the gap between the meal leaving and the dessert arriving that the guests' and McGrath's attention was drawn to little Ada, who was quietly emptying the sugar dispenser into a wondrous large mound of white granules, flattening them on the dark wood and then, with a licked first finger, drawing her name in the sugar.

The two neighboring aunts cleared their throats and looked toward their brother Wyston, who finally dropped his eyes to the artwork in front of his daughter's place and bellowed out of relief more than anger, "And what is that you are doing?"

"Drawing in the snow, Father," she said in her small, clear voice.

"That is not snow, dear, that is good sugar," said Aunt Ethel.

"No Aunt, it is snow. I have made it fall on to the table."

"Get up from the table and come to me," ordered her father.

The little girl could not get down from her chair with-

out help, and said so. This well-known fact infuriated her
father to an unexpected degree and he bellowed at her
with such force that a great spray of spit misted the air,
and Aunt Patricia, who was nearest him, withdrew her
hands from the table.

"You, child, will go to your room and not speak for
the rest of the day—as it seems you speak only to contradict your father and your aunts."

The child's face burned a fantastic red and a sweat that
prickled needles burst across her upper lip and forehead.
Her father had never spoken to her like this before; she
was accustomed to always being his favored pet.
McGrath himself was surprised by the force of his temper, aggravated as he was by the presence of the aunts and
the interruptions to his regular existence. But children
must be obedient, and Ada usually was, and when she was
not, her favor was coddled and coaxed pleasantly. On
this evening, spoken to in this manner, Ada's shame was
complete and she held her hands up across her face so
that none could look upon it. Her father lifted her down
from her chair and with her hands still over her face, and
tears now running down her cheeks, she stumbled out of
the dining room then on into the hall and up the main
stairs to her bedroom. Wyston straightened his jacket
and called after her, "And not to speak, mind you girlie."
He returned to the dining room to attempt to salvage
something of the evening meal, thinking nothing more
about his little daughter other than she would calm down
and, in the morning, be well.

In the safety of her bedroom the little girl threw herself across her small bed and, taking a bite-sized piece of pillow into her mouth to muffle her cries, prepared to sob. To her surprise no sobs came. And as the small child sat herself up, a darkness was in her eyes that was at once chilling and threatening. For a very long time the little girl sat, her hands folded tidily in her lap while her eyes, big, black, and cold, stared out toward the far wall. The child stayed like this, staring, unmoving, while all about her the room descended slowly into a shadowy darkness, then on into the night.

It was two days before it was noticed that the child still had not spoken and, to everyone's amazement, would not, even as she was ordered to say goodbye. After a week, when she still had not spoken, her father became concerned and called her into his study. His small dark-haired, dark-eyed daughter stood gravely in front of him. He looked at her and moved awkwardly in his upright chair. There was something eerily disquieting about those black eyes. The expression was part accusing, part aloof. Her little feet neatly lined themselves up against the edge of his Turkish rug.

"Ada," he said, "I have punished you and now this last week you have punished me." He looked at her and she looked back at him with a forgiving unmoving quiet. "In my calculation, we are even," and he added, "don't you think?" He bent forward so his big-featured face was on her level. "Are we even?"

Ada heard her father's kind voice and looked into the

face she loved so dearly, the face she had called "Beast," and despite her enormous love for him, and his utter devotion to her, she could not contradict the edict of her own small iron will. She, as firm as a window grille, would not speak.

The Beast settled into a position of equal parts admiration and fury toward the wee figure of his only daughter. Unwilling to take up arms against the child, he found a sport in making mock threats and quoting proverbs, the favorite of which, "The silent dog is the first to bite," he would repeat often; and soon daughter and father became even tighter, he in his mocking, admiring tolerance, she in her tiny child firmness. After another three years and two trips to Edinburgh specialists, it was understood, even by the maids who had in private shaken her to force a word, that little Ada did not speak. And her father's speeches became lore in the house. "It is a dark talent," he would say, "and the moment you take it into your head to stop breathing will be your last."

$\mathcal{B}$ Y the time she found herself jetsam washed up on a beach many thousands of miles from Aberdeen, Ada had long become accustomed to her own muteness, refusing to remember the "incident," but only knowing like a bird that flies south the reason was excellent, fundamental, and unquestionable, a part of the fabric of her being upon which everything else had been built.

Chapter 2

$\mathcal{I}$T was early morning. Beneath the forest canopy walked a party of fourteen Maori men and women and two *pakeha*—European men. The wetness, closeness, and darkness of the bush was so profound that the air itself seemed green, as at the bottom of the sea, while the sounds of birds and insects echoed loudly overhead. Alisdair Stewart walked stiffly, brushing the undergrowth roughly back, feeling as though the branches reached out for him, deliberately hindering his progress. He had been settled in New Zealand for a good many years now, and he had spent these same years fighting the bush. At first his land had provided a fine harvest of *kauri* trees—the massively tall, straight-limbed and near knotless trees so valued for ship's masts—-and since then Stewart had battled against the continual wanton regrowth of all manner of vine and fern. He thought sometimes that if he paused for even one day the bush would overtake all his labors, drowning his hard-won clearance in mossy green waves of luxuriant vegetation. When he ventured off his own land, it was his custom to carry with him an axe to clear a sensible path. The bush, like the Maori people who inhabited it, needed to be brought to order. Stewart felt, however, that to greet his new wife bearing an axe like a laborer was hardly appropriate, and so today he did without.

Alisdair Stewart was a tall, even-featured man who in his youth, and still now as he aged, was considered handsome by most women who knew him, dashing by his aunts and sisters, and he was not above summoning up a flicker of vanity as he considered how he might appear. He staggered and slowed to a stop, taking off his mud-spattered top hat. His fair hair and face were wet with perspiration and humidity. Taking a silver comb from his pocket and dragging it through his hair, he tugged at the tight, ill-fitting suit—a suit he had worn but twice in the past decade—which he had insisted on wearing for this long walk to meet his wife. To meet his wife! Stewart felt himself pale at the thought. Once again, for what must have been the hundredth time, he dug into his pocket to retrieve the small oval-framed daguerreotype of the woman he would shortly be meeting. She looks calm, he reassured himself not for the first time, sturdy. Ada, he said silently, turning the name over in his mind. Ada, my wife.

George Baines, the other white man in the party, paused to watch as Alisdair Stewart gazed at the daguerreotype. Baines himself appeared the opposite of Stewart: as short and knotted with muscle as the other was tall and lean; as eccentrically dressed in loose, color-ful clothing as the other was unsuitably formal; as calm and shy as the other was harried and nervous. Baines asked, "Shall we stop?" but Stewart, preoccupied, did not hear. Baines stared at Stewart; he found this man impossible to understand, with his daguerreotype and his unknown wife, his sealed rigidities. "Shall we stop?" Again, Stewart did not reply. Baines moved quickly after the Maoris, calling out, "*Tai hoa! Me tatari tatou . . . me tutatou i konei*—Wait! We are stopping . . . we're stopping." But as he turned back he saw Alisdair Stewart take one last secret look at the daguerreotype, tilting the oval frame toward the light so he could catch his own reflection. Suddenly determined, Stewart pressed forward, beating back his apprehension as he pushed through the trees. "We must get on," he said firmly.

The Maoris looked at Baines, bemused. One of their number turned to follow Stewart, now striding ahead. "*Aue tepatupaiarehe!*—the fairy people, what can you expect?" he said.

ONCE the company broke free from the grasp of the bush onto the hard sand of the beach their progress became considerably faster, even jaunty. They formed a ragged crowd, the Maoris dressed in peculiar and individual fashion, combining both traditional and European clothes worn in every manner possible. Like Alisdair Stewart, two of the Maori men wore top hats, but theirs were decorated with feathers and beads. Another two shared one pair of shoes.

As he crossed the sand, Stewart perceived a collection of boxes and crates in the distance. With rising panic he thought that the crates had been abandoned and that no people kept their company. There was no sign of a ship moored in the wide bay. But as he drew nearer he saw the little white bubble of what could only be a shelter. As the Maoris began to poke and kick at the boxes, Stewart approached the tiny enclosure. He brought himself up short when he understood that it was constructed from a petticoat; sticking out from beneath the white cotton was a small, stockinged foot.

The noise of the arriving party woke both Ada and Flora. Ada brought herself upright with a start, she could hear men's voices and they were speaking in a strange tongue. She straightened Flora's hair and adjusted her own, the tight plaits had not loosened during the long night. When a brown face ringed with long black curls suddenly lifted the cloth and peered in at them, Flora clutched her mother. To their relief they heard a distinct voice rise above the clamor: "Miss McGrath, Alisdair Stewart."

Outside the little tent, Stewart took off his hat and automatically combed his hair yet again, patting it against his forehead where it lay in thick, damp furrows, all the time thinking that this was an inauspicious beginning to his much-planned and dwelt-upon marriage. "You'll have to wake yourself. I've got men here to carry your things."

Taking deep breaths to still her agitated heart, Ada gave Flora a reassuring glance. To come all this way, and then be found sheltering inside one's petticoat; Ada felt no embarrassment, possessing no false sense of modesty, only trepidation and impatience for her new life. She struggled out backwards from under the hoops, pulling down her tightly fitted jacket as she came, hurriedly placing her bonnet over her hair. There seemed a great profusion of people; many men with brown skin stood and stared, and women too had gathered near to pluck at her clothes. Aboard ship Ada had heard many tales about the savage people of New Zealand, how they were warlike, fierce, seafaring cannibals. And here they were, all around her. Many of their faces were decorated with intricate markings; even the other white man present had a similar small design on his forehead and nose, his curly hair framed by a straw hat that he wore as though at a picnic. Some of the Maori men had bare arms and legs, their hairless chests and stomachs exposed to the breeze. Ada lowered her eyes as she did not know where to look, what might next appear. She had never seen unclothed human flesh before, apart from her own, her child's. The men and women wore shells around their necks, beaded and carved earrings, bands of color in their hair, and they walked back and forth along the beach freely, unencumbered by boots, hoops, and other fashionable European restraints. As she lifted her head slowly to look at these people, they stared back, uttering loud comments Ada could not understand. One of them, a large and solid woman dressed in a rough burlap shirt and skirt, long black hair hanging loose around her shoulders, came close by and reached out a hand. Ada stared downward, fumbling with her bonnet ribbon while the woman, Waimara, stroked her cheek. "*Te komaa hoki . . . ano nei he Anahera enei?*—Look how pale—like angels." It seemed the Maori people were as astounded by the two women as they by them. Flora, smitten with shyness, hid behind her mother's skirt.

Presented with her husband for the first time, Ada McGrath felt overcome and could not bring herself to look at Alisdair Stewart, just as he could not bring himself to look upon her. "Well," he spoke forcefully against the wind, attempting to conceal his awkwardness, "I see you have a good many boxes. I'd like to know what is in each." As he spoke Ada felt her skirt suddenly lift. There were two young men lying on the sand, prodding the cloth of her petticoat with a stick as though Ada were a strange animal. One of them pointed at her feet and gestured as if he were holding Ada's shoe in his hand. "*Te monohi hoki!*—So small!" Ada gasped and kicked her foot out to the side, unused to such bold scrutiny.

Stewart looked at Ada, puzzled. "CAN—YOU—HEAR—ME?" he intoned loudly. Ada nodded and looked directly at him, her eyes cold, insulted by his slow speech and its deliberate volume. The Maori women had dismantled the tent and were now gamboling along, one of them wearing the crinoline cage over her own tattered skirt.

"Well, that is good, yes, that is good. Good." He smiled then and searched Ada McGrath's face for some sign of comprehension. Alisdair Stewart felt unnerved by his wife's lack of response. He had expected, even hoped for, shyness, modesty, but had not envisaged such starchy solemnity. He stopped smiling and, patting his hair yet again, walked to the nearest crate. Several of the Maori party followed behind Stewart while one of them closely mimicked each of his movements. "What's in here?" he asked, indicating a large trunk.

Ada pointed to the inscription on the box: CROCKERY AND POTS. She had packed under the careful supervision of her maiden aunts; all the trunks had been labeled meticulously, and in her bag she carried an inventory.

"Oh yes, so it is," Stewart said, leaning over to survey the writing, which one of the Maori men dabbed with his fingers as though it might speak. "Crockery . . ." Stewart stole a sideways glance at Ada from under his hat. He spoke without thinking: "You're small. I never thought you would be small." At that, Ada seemed to shrink even smaller.

"And this one?" Stewart asked as he strode toward the biggest crate on the beach. "It is very large. What is in it, then, a bedstead?"

Everyone gathered round the crate and when someone knocked upon it, the piano produced a reverberating echo. Ada took from the folds of her jacket the silver notepad and pencil she wore round her neck, but before she could write a reply, Flora spread her arms protectively across the top of the splintery wood and spoke to her new stepfather for the first time. "It is my mother's piano," she said, pushing a rope away as her mother moved anxiously to her side.

Stewart turned away without comment, as though Flora had not spoken. He strode across the sand, addressing the other European man: "Baines, tell them to carry in pairs. Take all the boxes, the table, and the suitcases." He waved one hand dismissively at the baggage. Ada watched from a distance while the two white men paused and drew near. She could not hear what was being said.

"What do you think?" Stewart kept his voice low, nodding toward Ada. George Baines considered for a moment, the salt breeze tickling his face and hair as he gazed over at the woman.

"She looks tired," he said eventually.

"She's stunted, that's one thing," Stewart answered abruptly. He marched away then but Baines continued to watch as Ada signed to her daughter in a distracted, determined way. The child looked puzzled and, as Baines looked on, Ada opened her notepad again and wrote upon it.

Flora carried the white slip of paper to Stewart. "The piano?" the note read.

"Oh no, it can't come now," Stewart said decisively.

"It must," affirmed Flora. "She wants it to come."

"Yes, and so do I," he spoke plainly to the child as they walked back to where Ada and the piano stood. "But there are too few of us here to carry it now," he explained, adding loudly to Ada, "Too heavy."

Ada, fear rising in her breast, quickly wrote another note and handed it to her husband. "I NEED THE PIANO."

"You mean you don't want your kitchenware or your clothing? Is that what you mean?" Stewart asked in disbelief.

Ada signed to Flora, who translated, "We can't leave the piano."

"Let's not discuss this any further. I'm very pleased that you've arrived safely." Stewart began to speak quite formally, hoping to infuse a note of welcome into his voice and to prevent any further discussion on the subject.

"Mother wants to know if they could come back directly for it . . ."

Stewart, unable to believe he was being interrupted by a child, ignored Flora's question and addressed his wife: "Could I apologize for the delay which I regret was caused . . ."

As he spoke Ada kept signing rapidly. Flora watched her mother and then interrupted Stewart again in a voice that was both insistent and strident, ". . . after they have taken the other things?" Stewart looked vexed, his mouth hanging slightly open. He turned away as though to control his temper.

The Maoris began to find the situation amusing, add-

ing to his growing discomfort. *"Kia tupato . . . kuu pukuri-
ribia . . . a te raho Maroke*—Watch it, old dry-balls is getting
touchy," said Kamira, one of the older men. All the Maoris laughed, leaving Stewart with a taut, uncomprehending smile on his face.

The matter of the piano was now closed. Stewart felt
he had been humiliated, challenged by these two small
women who ought to have bowed to his judgment. The
piano was unneeded and heavy, and, furthermore, if he
were to give way now to their demands it would be an
unfortunate precedent. They must accept his authority.

The whole episode had unsettled Stewart deeply. The
meeting had not gone the way he had long dreamed; he
had imagined something very different. He had even
thought that at some stage he would kiss her hand, but
somehow that now seemed strange and impossible.
"Might I suggest you prepare for a difficult journey," he
said to Ada brusquely, glancing about. "The bush will
tear clothes and the mud is deep in places."

With that, Stewart departed, leaving Ada still standing
beside her piano. Flora edged close by her mother, patting her hand in an effort to provide comfort. Ada
watched as Stewart strode toward the Maoris, who had
busied themselves collecting the shellfish they called *pipis*.
She could not accept this turn of events. She had brought
the piano so far, all those sea miles, months, and days. It
was part of herself; a solid incarnation of her past; she
could not leave it on the beach.

"What are they doing?" Stewart shouted at Baines as some young men raced each other into the sea. "We don't have time for that."

𝒜 FEW moments later everything that could be had been collected and the party began to walk toward the cliffs, toward the seemingly impregnable bush, away from the shining, tumbling ocean. Alisdair Stewart did not speak to Ada McGrath, but told Baines to instruct the two women to follow. Ada, still caught between the rolling waves and the sea of forest, knew she had no choice. Baines indicated the direction and a narrow path opened before them as they came to the edge of the trees. Her eyes full of tears, her small white face clouded with anger and resentment, Ada took Flora's hand and set off, leaving Baines struck silent by her show of emotion.

After climbing up the long hill the transport party reached a point on the cliff where Ada was afforded a sudden view of the solitary piano against its backdrop of churning sea. She looked down on it, alone in its crate on the wide, comfortless strand, the tide approaching its legs once again. Without her piano she felt very far from home, even farther than she had the night before. She felt voiceless, silenced in a way that had nothing to do with the inability to speak. For several minutes Ada gazed out over the beach, emotions flooding her mind as she struggled to subdue the urge to defy her husband in the first few moments of their marriage. She gripped Flora's hand, anchoring herself to the only thing she had left in the world. She would return, she told herself, she would find a way to retrieve the piano from the beach.

Chapter 3

$\mathcal{A}$s Ada McGrath grew, so did the mythic glory of her stubborn will, and she shouldered it like a prickly but glorious shawl. It was her. As a twelve-year-old she was still tiny, neat, and perfect—not beautiful but alluring. The boldness of her dark-eyed look could be alarming, and she frightened the more timid maids with her steady gaze.

The twelve-year-old Ada liked to do three things: to read, to make things beautiful, which generally meant to polish, and to play the piano. Of the three, the piano was her favorite, and in this her father indulged her. He had bought it as a wedding anniversary present for his young wife Cecilia; she too had loved the instrument with a passion that could have been unseemly in other circumstances. Wyston and Cecilia had only two anniversaries together, and the second had been celebrated with especial joy. Cecilia played the piano every day for the last six months of her confinement and Wyston chanced to joke that he believed the baby might be born singing.

The baby was born, but no one sang, as the labor had been long and frightening, and had left Cecilia weakened. Wyston busied himself around the estate, roistering about the house, placing demands on anxious staff when he knew he should be quiet and calm. The baby, a girl—they named her Ada after Cecilia's own mother—seemed well enough, red-faced and mewling, but the mother continued to fade. Three weeks later she was dead. Wyston was left on his own with the baby. And the piano to remind him of his wife.

It was a Broadwood piano, a boxed grand, made of rosewood. The top panels were carved into delicate and intricate floral shapes and underneath was laid a deep red satin. The legs were fluted and curled into fists or, as Ada had it, lion's paws. The piano sounded best with its top panels put aside so the harplike strings could ring out freely. Under the strings was a delicate inlay of blond wood and tiny inscriptions that the pianomaker had made to guide him in his work. The felts were black and there was an additional layer of thin red felt along one edge. It pleased Ada to watch when McGregor, the tuner, worked on her instrument, to see how many pieces could be removed—the lid, the top panels and each and every key singularly by slotting them carefully in and out. McGregor complimented the piano, and little Ada would blush with pleasure as if the piano itself was her mother and it was she that was complimented on her exquisite shape, design, and tone. No one ever referred to the piano as having belonged to Ada's mother, but Ada knew it had been hers and, somehow, since she had no memory of her mother, as she played Ada conjured a soft, warm figure composed of music and polished wood and called it "Cecilia."

"It's as clear as a voice," McGregor said one day as he worked on the piano. He visited the McGrath house regularly for tuning, due to the damp, harsh climate and the amount the instrument was played. He looked at Ada as she gravely guarded the dismantled pieces, adding, "and just as well wee one, just as well, with that closed trap of yours. Eh? What are you holding on to—a mouse? Is it? Come on, open up and you'll hear it squeak."

Ada's faced clouded, her eyes darkened, and she bent her head as if to aim her eyes more particularly at him. Seeing he was embarrassing the girl he stopped teasing and worked silently. After Ada had passed each of the panels to the tuner, the tuner had admiringly slotted them together, saying, "Ingeniously simple, look at that." He turned to Ada and took her hand, looking into her eyes. "Have you a secret my small one, a big secret, something frightening you saw?" Little Ada felt the glorious, solemn seriousness of the moment and her eyes filled with tears as they might if an anthem had been sung, so when she shook her head, the tuner squinted and let her pull her little hand out of his. But he remained convinced of his instincts. "There is more to her silence than will ever be spoken," he told the kitchen maids.

"Don't be a simple fool," the youngest replied. "It's only her dark little ways. She's been nothing but spoilt ever since she were first born."

Before playing her Broadwood the child closed the dining room door to the kitchen, and that door into the hall. She closed the hall door, the sitting room door, and the door from the sitting room that led into a large paneled parlor that had been her mother's workroom, and there she would sit no less than two hours and some days for four or five hours. She had no formal training, but could pick and play any tune she had heard thereabouts.

Later that month, a dressmaker was called to the house and fitted Ada with her first long skirt, corset, and hoop. On the same day her father made the piano a present to her. And she, as a present to him, played his favorite pieces.

To see this tiny figure climb up onto the stool adjusted with two large books and bow over the keyboard, serious and purposeful, filled Wyston McGrath with awe. The playing was simple but surprisingly fetching, passionate, musical. It impressed and embarrassed him that she should sway and even effect eye-closing to find her way. He was sensitive enough not to abuse this privilege by ever requesting her to play for guests, maids, or any others. But it did serve the purpose of fixing in his mind the idea that she might be given coaching. Someone who could teach her in music and perhaps act as a general tutor.

THE journey through the bush seemed interminable. The day grew very warm and humid, clothes tightened and turned sticky with perspiration, heavy with mud. Ada marveled at the exotic abundance of the bush as they moved slowly through it; all variety of filmy frond, bracken, and moss seemed to grow in this country, new trees sprouting out of decaying, dead trees, all intertwined in a jumble of thick and trailing vines, leaves, and roots. The flat green face of the forest was transformed within by filters of sunlight, revealing a shifting kaleidoscope of color, from the palest new curl of fern to the purple-black gloss of the gigantic palms. Bare brown feet squelched through the mud up ahead; it was evident to Ada that they were being led by the Maoris, and by the man George Baines who seemed to know the direction as well as acting as interpreter for Stewart. The way was not easy, and Ada and Flora struggled in their dainty boots and cumbersome skirts.

Alisdair Stewart pushed on ahead of his new wife and her child, not daring to look back, his mind full of contradiction. At last she had arrived, but she was different from what he had imagined. He chided himself; when he had learned that she was mute he had bestowed upon her the qualities of a silent nun, pious, biddable, beautiful, and infinitely respectful and grateful toward himself. Of course she was none of these things. She was a mail-order bride, and he had been a fool for expecting a quiescent saint.

Nor did Alisdair Stewart fulfil Ada McGrath's expectations, although hers had been, assuredly, much lower. One is not sold across the sea to find oneself mistress to a princely master; this land had no princes, she already knew that, despite Flora's stories. Ada pushed her boots firmly down into the mud, determined not to slip, no longer caring about the fate of her skirts. The Maori men rolled their trousers up above their knees and the women wisely tucked up their clothing. Ada could see Flora struggling up ahead, her little legs not quite long enough, her breath quick and labored, her blue tartan skirt dragging in the mud continuously. At least the child was stifled by the boredom of the ship no longer, Ada reflected, this world and the people in it so strange and different.

Flora clambered over another rock. In this fresh world with a new stepfather, a whole new life, Flora's first impression was one of mud: muddy legs and boots and feet. She had never been allowed to play in the soft gray mud at home, but here she was expected to crawl right through it in her best traveling dress. Flora found it all most enjoyable. Like Ada, Flora was possessed of a fine curiosity, and during the long sea voyage had disengaged herself from the past with a childish ease. She had her mother with her, that was enough. The party came abruptly to a halt in a clearing. Baines worked his way to the front. The Maoris were talking.

"*E aha tenei*—What is it?" Baines spoke quietly.

The Maori leader, Hone, his face partially covered with the deep grooves of ritual tattooing, replied, "*E hinga te Koroua ra a Pitama i konei*—Old man Pitama died here."

He pointed through the trees. *"Kare noa Kia hikina te Tapu*—The *Tapu* hasn't been lifted."

Stewart struggled up to the front. He ignored the Maori and spoke directly to Baines. "What's the matter?"

Hone started to explain but Stewart interrupted, speaking exclusively to Baines, "Why are they stopping?"

"Someone died here. It's Tapu." Baines spoke to Stewart softly.

"But we came down this way, didn't we? I'm sure we did." Stewart was insistent, irritated by the unnecessary delay.

The Maoris continued their discussion. *Tapu* was sacred ground, holy. Hone suggested that someone go to look for another track.

"They want more money," Stewart griped. "They are trying to make two days out of it?"

"No, no," Baines replied, "they know another track— to the side of this."

While the men argued over the route, Ada and Flora looked for a dry place to sit and catch their breath. All at once the bush seemed claustrophobic, as though it had begun closing over their heads the moment they stopped moving, like disturbed water rippling into stillness once again. Ada sat down on the crumbling trunk of a fallen tree, Flora climbing up beside her. Ada sensed a melancholy dripping ooze all around them, beneath the bird song and the breeze in the tree canopy overhead. It was most oppressive.

On either side of Ada and Flora sat two Maori

women, the older Waimara (whom Ada had noticed on the beach in her burlap shirt and wide skirt) and a younger woman. Ada felt intimidated by their inscrutable presence, like the presence of the bush. With their unbound hair and loose clothes they seemed comfortable in their bodies, in their flesh, weighty and imperturbable in a manner that could not have been more foreign to Ada in her bonnet and tightly laced stays. Waimara took Ada's silver notecase in her broad hands and examined it from every angle as it dangled on its chain, while the younger woman stealthily began to draw Ada's shawl out of her lap into her own. She passed it quickly behind to Waimara who placed the shawl around her own shoulders, smiling with triumph and luxury. Ada, aware of what was happening, stared stiffly ahead, unable to react. She felt as though she had been tricked, and she dared not look at the older woman as she arranged and then rearranged the shawl on her broad shoulders.

Meanwhile the other woman was making a dignified and futile attempt to wipe the light freckles from Flora's face. Flora submitted, dolefully.

Just as Ada was beginning to despair, they arrived at the place where Alisdair Stewart lived. It was raining heavily now, and the sky glowered dark and low to the sodden ground. In the middle of a muddy clearing littered with the charred and blackened skeletons of trees stood the house that Stewart had built himself with wooden planks he had split from *kauri* trees with his own axe and sweat—he proudly called it a house, and it was a house compared to other structures in the area. But where others saw a swamp of mud and charcoal, Alisdair Stewart had a vision: his own estate. Dreaming of polite gardens and lawns, Stewart had razed the bush around the house, utilizing the technique of slash and burn. He had raised himself up out of the cloying mud; his new family would drink their tea from china teacups that afternoon.

But to Ada and Flora the house was nothing more than a crude cabin in the midst of a barren graveyard; in the rain everything was black and gray. Although they were glad to have their journey over, both Ada and Flora felt a dark foreboding that it should end in such a drear place.

The Maoris dumped all the boxes and suitcases on the porch; Alisdair Stewart paid them, and they left. George Baines had already departed for his own property, farther up the valley. Ada found herself shivering.

Stewart escorted Ada and Flora through the few rooms, the kitchen, the pantry, the parlor. It was simple but clean—Stewart's Aunt Morag had helped him prepare for his new wife's arrival—and there were a few plain pictures on the walls. A stocky wood-burning stove dominated the kitchen, and a cold meal had been laid on the table. The journey had calmed Stewart's irritation, and he took obvious pride in his house. When he showed them the two bedrooms he cleared his throat shyly and said, "Make yourselves comfortable," without suggesting in which room they might put their things. He pointed through the window to a wooden platform several feet out into the yard. "That's the well and pump there. As you can see I have planted a peach, a pear, and an apple; they each bear a little fruit now, in the late summer. There is much to do." He turned to look at Ada hopefully. "I trust you will find everything to your satisfaction. I must tend to a few chores before I retire for the night. Tomorrow I will show you my—"he paused, clearing his throat, "—our—property." With that, he nodded, full of expectation and doubt once again, showed his strained smile, exchanged his top hat for a more workmanlike cap, and strode off through the moonlight.

Flora sat down on the bed, her eyes very wide. "I don't want to stay here."

Ada signed, "We must."

"I'm not staying."

"Where will you go?" asked Ada.

Flora stood and went to the window, Ada behind her. They looked out at the night, at the dark place to which they had come. "Mumma, where might the privy be?"

𝒯HE next day the rain continued unabated. When Ada and Flora rose, they found that Alisdair Stewart had already gone. They had both slept heavily, still rocking with the ship. There was bread and preserves on the table. They ate, then Ada began to unpack, going first to the trunk that contained toys for Flora, her dollies, the dollies' wardrobe. She had assumed that the bedroom that Stewart had left them standing in the night previously was to be theirs. The other was more masculine, full of his things. It did not occur to Ada that Stewart might well expect his room to be hers as well.

Stewart arrived back at midday. His boots and trousers were thick with mud, and he smelt of hard work. He retired behind the curtain of what was the bathroom, and while he used the fine basin and jug he had carried from Scotland, he informed Ada, "My aunt, her companion and the Reverend will be arriving shortly." Even as he spoke Ada looked out the window to see three people, all tall and round-shouldered, making their way through the mud and driving rain, laden with hampers and baskets.

Alisdair Stewart's Aunt Morag was a large woman with a long face, marked by a dark mole below one corner of her mouth. When she smiled her face was friendly, but she did not smile often, and to the casual observer she appeared stern indeed. Nessie, Morag's companion, was younger, of a similar build, as if somehow modeled on Morag, though her round face was unlined, not yet set in its expression. Their dresses were severe and practical in cut, plain cloth and simple lace collars with no regard for current fashion, no thick tartan, no costly velvet trimmings like those Ada favored, and they both wore lace caps to cover their hair, Nessie's white, Morag's black.

They smiled, nodded, and clucked, pleased at last to make acquaintance with Morag's nephew's new wife. Ada and her daughter Flora were scrutinized carefully, and Aunt Morag pronounced them both very small and light, smiling and saying, "We'll have to make sure Alisdair thickens you up—it is a hard life we live here, we must keep strength."

"The only vicar between here and Otaki," announced the Reverend Septimus Campbell, Morag's younger brother, when introduced.

The proclaimed purpose of this visitation was to arrange for a wedding photograph of Morag's nephew and his new wife. While Ada was out of the room the Reverend began squealing and chasing Aunt Morag, the mock wedding dress stuck partway up his plump arms, his little round spectacles askew. "Septimus," Morag berated the befrocked Reverend, "now take that off. Take that off." Morag shrieked as they thundered around the table, shaking the house. "Watch your feet!"

"Watch your feet!" shouted Nessie, who had developed the habit of repeating the last few of all Morag's words, an echo Morag ignored.

"Oh, you'll tear it. Stop it!" cried Morag; "Stop it!" echoed Nessie. But the Reverend persisted, and their game continued amid whoops of excitement and pleasure. Ada found the scene alarming, reared as she had been an only child among adults in a house known for its silence. She and Flora retreated into the quietude of the bedroom.

Soon Aunt Morag and Nessie followed Ada, bringing

with them the wedding dress, a backless frock with ties like a surgical gown used time and again as a photographic prop. It was only then that Ada understood they meant to fit her with it.

"Lift—your—arm—up," Aunt Morag said slowly, presuming Ada deaf. "Arm down." Flora stood beside the mirror and watched as they pinned a long, tatty veil on her mother's head. The little girl's ordinarily bright expression darkened; she sat on the bed sulkily. Since their arrival, all attention had been focused on her mother; no one seemed interested in her. Flora was not ordinarily given to petulance, but this was a special occasion.

"Beautiful," remarked Morag of the dress. "The lace is most fragile."

Flora spoke suddenly: "My real father was a famous German composer." Aunt Morag and Nessie stopped what they were doing and stared at the little girl who seemed to swell slightly with their attention.

"They met when my mother was an opera singer in Luxembourg."

Ada signed to Flora, a single movement yet vehement: "That's enough."

"Why?" whispered Flora, her bright storytelling face crumpling. Ada looked away. As Morag and Nessie began primping the lace again, Flora crossed her arms, vexed. "I want to be in the photograph," she said with a childish pout. It was evidently far from appropriate for

Alisdair Stewart to have the fatherless Flora in his wedding photograph; it was to be just the happy couple.

$\mathcal{T}$HE relationship of Flora to her mother was one of mirrorlike closeness, a kind of symbiosis. Ada was a stranger here and Flora was her mediator, a task she fell to with natural passion. Like Ada at her age, Flora was a charming, precocious child, accustomed to the company of adults, but Flora was a light-hearted girl, less solemn than Ada had been.

The child had a talent as a storyteller; in the family she was known for her tall tales, which Ada and Wyston indulgently thought of as imaginative wanderings, and the staff and the neighbors called lies. It was as though Flora in her imagining was compensating for both the mysteries and secrets of the adult household in which she lived, and her own mother's terrible silence. Flora was the main reason that Ada had agreed to her father's marriage plans, as she saw the wisdom of taking the girl away to a new life. Maybe in a different place, a new country full of much-heralded opportunity, the past would not matter so much. When Ada had doubts on the journey, she told herself she had married for Flora, although the truth of the matter was that she was leaving Scotland almost as much for herself.

$\mathcal{I}$T was still raining when they were ready for the photograph to be taken. A thick mizzle of showers fell across the distant bush, the whole valley was wraithed in mist. Nessie held an umbrella over Ada as they made their way along the plank-walk to where the camera had been set up in front of two chairs. They both slid, their feet skidding beneath their skirts. "I almost slipped on the plank, they've gotten very greasy," Nessie informed Stewart as they reached the platform. There were other settlers there to help out, or, rather, to see the new bride for themselves. Alisdair Stewart himself was looking intently through the camera at Ada, who sat holding a drooping bouquet in front of the curtained false backdrop depicting a sunny landscape more like Tuscany than this dreich place. Stewart came to sit beside Ada, pausing to take off his hat and comb his hair back once again, full of pride at his new status as husband and pleased at Ada's charming aspect in the lace gown. He turned to smile at his wife, but just then lightning slashed across the sky and they were engulfed by blinding torrents of rain. With a sharp intake of breath, Ada stared at the camera grimly, not hearing the photographer's fey words of encouragement.

$\mathcal{A}$ CANDLE lit the bedroom, illuminating Aunt Morag's uncontainable curiosity. She was glad to have been given the task of minding the child; alone with her, she might be able to elicit some useful facts regarding Flora's birth and her mother's shame.

"I thought she met your father in Luxembourg," Morag said to Flora.

"Well, yes, in Austria, where he conducted the Royal Orchestra . . ."

Morag frowned, torn between belief and scepticism. The child was getting her facts confused. "And where did they get married?" Morag glanced out the window to see if anyone was coming.

"In an enormous forest, with real fairies as bridesmaids each holding a little elf's hand." Flora's voice became rich and dramatic.

Morag sat back a little, regarding Flora with kindly disapproval. She smoothed back her hair.

Flora, sensing Morag's incredulity, said, "No, I tell a lie, it was in a small country church, near the mountains."

"Which mountains are those, dear?"

"The Pyrenees."

"Oh, I've never been." Morag leaned forward, once again suspending all disbelief.

"Mother used to sing songs in German and her voice would echo across the valleys . . . That was before the accident."

"Oh," said Morag, "what happened?" Morag was eager to hear more, for the sake of her nephew Alisdair, of course. "One day when my mother and father were singing together in the forest, a great storm blew up out of nowhere. But so passionate was their singing that they did not notice, nor did they stop as the rain began to fall, and when their voices rose for the final bars of the duet a great bolt of lightning came out of the sky and struck my father so that he lit up like a torch. And at the same moment my father was struck dead, my mother was struck dumb!" The child lowered her voice in revelation. "She—never—spoke—another—word."

"Ohh," said Morag, truly shocked, having entered fully into the gaudy world of Flora's imagination. "Oh dear! Not another word?" Flora shook her head. "From the shock, yes it would be," Morag conjectured.

But Flora's compelling tale was interrupted by the return of the wedding party, who had been drenched by rain, exactly like the couple in the story. Aunt Morag, her face puckered with tragedy, got up and went over to help Nessie take off Ada's long, faux wedding gown, now heavy with water. "Terrible . . . terrible . . ." she murmured, looking upon Ada in a new light. But Ada, soaked to the bone, and distressed by this mockery of a wedding, began to pull the gown from herself so aggressively that the ribbons and the fabric tore apart. Morag and Nessie tutted and fretted, but none of this was of any concern to Ada. Her thoughts were elsewhere. She crossed to the little window and stared anxiously out at the falling rain, her mind full of fear for her piano. None of the distractions of the day had served to stop her from dwelling on it. She imagined her piano on the beach, seawater swirling high around its carved legs, unprotected and embattled in the dark, wet night. Alisdair Stewart had not mentioned arranging for it to be transported. Ada felt sure that he was determined to leave it there on the sand, as though in denial of her past. There had to be some way for her to rescue it. She would find a way. .

As Flora was finishing her toast the next morning, Alisdair Stewart came into the bedroom. He picked up the sodden bundle of lace from the table—the wedding dress—then discarded it, annoyed. He watched the two women, hands dancing, absorbed in conversation. He felt an intruder, uneasy as much with their secret communication as with their femininity, irritated at his inability to participate in their intimacy. As he moved toward them, Flora and Ada separated, sitting up stiff-backed, as though at attention, the atmosphere changing perceptibly. Stewart knocked some hoops from where they hung on the partition, replacing them awkwardly.

"I have to go away for some days," he said, his tone apologetic. "There is some Maori land I am interested in, which I may buy very reasonably." Stewart looked down at his feet, embarrassed, shuffling. "I hope you will spend the time settling in, and perhaps, in some way, we could start again." He looked at Ada, hopefully, "Right?" He nodded, looking away shyly as Ada nodded back. "Should there be any problems, go to Mr. Baines, George Baines, whom you met. He lives a short distance up the valley—I've left a map."

Stewart left on horseback. Getting his new wife to settle in was proving more difficult than he had anticipated. Aunt Morag had been helpful yesterday, introducing Ada to the domestic chores they had agreed should be his new wife's domain: washing, carrying water, tending the fire, sewing, cooking, the vegetable garden, the chickens . . . the list had seemed long as Morag painstakingly went over it, although Ada had shown no dismay. He would have to give her time, he thought.

Once Alisdair Stewart had left, Ada could think of nothing but the piano. Already her life seemed colorless without it, the hours elongated with silence. As she went about her tasks—where had Stewart's aunt said the washing basin was at?—she conceived of a plan to ask Mr. Baines to take them to see if the instrument had yet been borne away by the tide. Baines had a kind face and a quiet manner, he might be agreeable. Ada studied the map Stewart had left on the kitchen table. She dressed Flora in her cloak and bonnet, and then, herself wearing a ruffled black coat that fitted her neatly and she thought might allow her more freedom to walk, they began the trek across the planks that served as a sporadic pavement over the mud, often stepping off and sinking deep into the mire again. Thicker, blacker, more fetid mud, Ada had never encountered.

Baines' hut sat in a clearing much brighter and leafier then the depressingly barren ground around the house of Alisdair Stewart. George Baines had felt no need to clear the native trees and plants off his property. There was bird song, and Ada noticed a parrotlike creature with bright green breast plumage, as though it had been plunged in dye. The rain had ceased. Sunlight fell down onto the steep thatched roof of George Baines' dwelling. A roan horse was tethered to one side of the hut.

Ada and Flora McGrath approached the door, which was cut in half like a stable door, the bottom portion standing open, and knocked. Flora crouched down to look inside and a pair of legs, clad only in long underwear, became visible. Flora stood up smartly and Baines answered the door. It was midmorning. Ada wondered at what time he considered full dress appropriate. She wrote a quick note on her silver notepad and handed it to him. George Baines turned it over, then, with a blank, unembarrassed look said, "I'm not able to read."

Ada, taken aback at this casual admission of an ignorance she found lamentable, signed to Flora.

"Please take us back to the beach where we landed," the girl translated.

Now it was Baines' turn to disguise shock. "I'm sorry," he said as Ada and Flora stared evenly at him. "I can't do that. I don't have the time." With that, he said good-bye and closed the door in their faces.

There being no one else to whom she could turn, Ada decided they would wait for Baines to come out of his house. She was determined: He had to help her. They sat directly in view of the door. Flora told Ada a story then, about a little house in a little clearing where an evil man lived. "When he comes out of his house, he collects the children who are lost, and he takes them back to his house with him. He gives them sweets to please them, to make them quiet and happy. He takes the children into his house where he has a roaring fire. Then he cooks them, one at a time. All the other children are made to watch. He cooks them very slowly. Their screams are very terrible. And then he eats them, one at a time, spitting out their bones on the floor. He is an evil man." Ada smiled at her child, half-listening, half-thinking about the piano, wondering when George Baines would come forth from his hut.

When Baines did emerge, carrying his jacket over his arm, the two women were still waiting with a great reserve of patience still to exploit. Baines was surprised to see them seated there so calmly, like two wood spirits come to plague him; as he stepped out they looked up at him expectantly. He was unsure what to make of their persistence.

"I—can't—take—you—there." He spoke to Ada in the slow manner which she detested. "I can't do it." Baines took the saddle from the porch rail and slung it on the horse, sneaking glances at the two women from behind the animal. Ada and Flora watched closely, not pleading, but stubborn, willing him to change his mind. To his eyes they seemed eerily alike, one a charming diminutive of the other. As he moved, their pale faces, framed by identical black bonnets, followed him, turning in unison. At length he acknowledged that he had no choice but to acquiesce, to give in to their determination. He felt that if he left them seated there, there they would remain and Baines did not relish the thought of these two watching him forever. So it was this dread, a little pity, and a slight curiosity that helped Baines to decide. He led them to the beach on his horse, making the journey much more swiftly than when the transport party had traveled loaded with the McGrath possessions.

Miraculously, the piano was still there, perched like an enormous piece of driftwood on the beach where they had left it, protected only by its crate and oilskins. Ada moved as quickly down the steep incline as she was able, her happy reunion hampered by her skirts and crinoline. Once there, she began to prise the box from the keyboard with her bare hands, tearing at the wood that was branded with her name, displaying a hunger and sudden impatience remarkable to George Baines. He helped her to fashion a primitive seat and then Ada began to play. The piano found its voice and Ada with it. It was as though she could breathe again. It was as though she had been freed.

The sky was thinly blue with long wisps of cloud that floated away on the afternoon. Baines watched as a great change came over Ada McGrath. Her whole composition altered. She closed her eyes and swayed as she played, her lips open in a half-smile. She was animated, joyful, radiant, not the dour, worried woman whom Baines had met earlier.

On the wet sand Flora stripped to her petticoats and, feeling light and free, did a wild dance of her own invention waving streamers of seaweed, inspired by her mother's happiness. She danced and ran, leapt and spun in time to Ada's playing. Baines had never seen women behave with such abandon. His attention was caught by Ada's emotional playing, and as he watched he found himself edging irresistibly closer to her as she bent, serene and glowing, over the keys.

She played rapid arpeggios and airy speeding trills, possessed of an unnameable undercurrent that tugged and stirred like the pull of the tide. George Baines was enthralled. He had never heard music like this, so filled with longing; he had never seen anyone play an instrument with such passionate absorption. He could not keep his eyes from the sight of this woman, lost in the sound of the music she played. It was a moment of great beauty, there on the sand, with the waves crashing and the seabirds circling overhead. Ada played and played, sometimes accompanied by Flora but mostly on her own, while George Baines still watched and listened. The music was unearthly, and the women, too, seemed otherworldly to Baines, like angels. Baines was moved, almost as if he might cry with pleasure at such beauty and rarity.

While Ada played, Flora determined to make a seahorse and she started by fashioning tiny creatures using four or five shells, but Baines said, no, she must make a huge creature, big enough for them to see from the clifftop. He allowed himself to be coerced into collecting shells and placing them as the child demanded. It was strange for him to be a part of this girl's fancy, strange and entrancing to be alone on the beach with these two women. The music made it hard for him to move, for he didn't so much listen to it with his ears, but with his whole body so that it ran through him and he was stilled into hearing and stilled into silence.

As they worked, Flora told Baines stories about their journey, their great trip across the blue riband. "And there were flying fish and they landed in our cooking pot," Flora said. George Baines listened, but he had only half an ear for Flora's stories. Ada's music filled his head.

As the shadows began to lengthen on the sand, Baines collected the boards discarded from the crate. He was not able to transport the piano for them on his own, yet he was concerned to protect it. As Ada noticed Baines coming toward her, obviously intending that they should leave, her mood darkened and she continued playing stubbornly for some time until, abruptly, she stopped, closing the lid over the keys. In sudden black spirits, she replaced her cape and bonnet, and they began the journey home.

Chapter 4

So while Wyston McGrath resolved when Ada was twelve that she should have piano tutoring, and told his plans to his accountant, his lawyer Mr. Beadsley, McGregor the piano tuner, and anyone and everyone at the drinking house, it was yet four years before Delwar Haussler, a twenty-three-year-old man, was met at Edinburgh Station and from there taken by coach to the McGrath estate.

His appointment was finalized not by Wyston McGrath but by Beadsley and the accountant, who took the plan into their own hands and advertised with several minor universities, thinking that that would render a cheaper and more humble type of person. There was but one reply, so the decision was made of itself, and Mr. Haussler agreed to begin teaching music and French on a two-month trial basis.

The estate at which the young man arrived was not the same proud, well-kept farm into which Ada had been born. The gate no longer closed, as one side had fallen off its hinge, and the drive up to the house was deeply rutted and potted with holes. McGrath, who had been so particular, seemed not to notice the decay; he treated it with the same benevolent tolerance with which he accepted his advancing age, feeling it natural that the property, like himself, should run down. And, as with all things he did not like, he had the knack of turning the other way and, childlike, imagining the problem gone. So as the farm's debts increased, he looked less and less at the accounts, until he refused to look at them at all. His accountant, Pike, a wise and kind man with eight children of his own, understood McGrath but sought also to protect McGrath's small daughter, for it was clear to all who did view the accounts that the estate would be bankrupted, and Pike feared for this child, who was said not to speak and could not earn a living. He persuaded McGrath to set up a trust fund for the child's dowry and education, a pocket of money that could not be attached to the fate of the property. So it was out of this fund that Delwar Haussler was to be paid.

Delwar arrived too late to meet his young pupil, and as he sat in the third-story room that was drafty, dirty even, the whole romance of his expedition was beginning to wane. For one thing he had not accounted for how cold it would be this far north, nor for the cheerlessness of the Scots whom he had imagined as hearty and friendly.

Delwar's first language was English, and while his father's family was originally German, neither he nor his father, a Lutheran pastor, had ever been to that country.

He was the third son and had two sisters, one older and one younger. Delwar wanted to be an artist, but his understanding of the career was fanciful, and he was successful only in its outward appearance. He wore his hair long with a velvet cap, a purple sash waistcoat, and a black frock coat that flapped dramatically in the wind. The coat had been made by his sisters and had a peculiarity of cut in that it was very tight across the chest and the collar sat two inches further down on the right side than the left. Delwar was touched by his sisters' effort and announced the oddities in design as original and distinctive additions. He was well loved by them, and they were envious of the Scottish girl who was to be the sole recipient of his attentions.

For the first week Delwar did not meet Ada. On the third day it was explained by McGrath that his daughter was very shy and unused to people, but she had agreed to spend time in the music room next week. Until then he should entertain himself as he pleased, play her piano, and in general settle in.

The first day of the second week Delwar came down into the music room and was surprised to see her already waiting; a tiny, perfectly dressed girl who looked twelve but whom he knew to be sixteen. Her expression was serious, almost stern, and her choice of dress was likewise severe yet of very good cloth and style. The white lace at her collar and cuffs was delicate, and it touched him that she too was so fragile, with her tiny hands and long slim neck. A perfect, proud miniature of an adult.

As Delwar moved forward to say hello, she unlatched a slim metal box that hung from a ribbon around her neck and removed a silver pencil attached to the side. Inside the box were small perfectly fitted pieces of cream paper, and onto the top sheet she wrote briefly and passed it to Delwar, carefully stepping back to her original position by the table at the far end of the room. On the piece of paper was written, "I do not speak."

For two weeks Delwar was unable to persuade Ada to move from the tableside, but he considered it progress that in the second week she left the room and returned carrying a dining chair that she placed beside the table and sat on.

Despite the oddness of the situation he was surprised to find himself chatty and comfortable, so that he carried on both sides of their conversation in between performances on the piano. All requests to Ada to play were met with deep blushes, a bowed head, and, on an early occasion, a walk out of the room. Delwar himself was an average pianist. He had good feeling and was well measured; he had a wide appreciation but knew by heart only the beginnings of pieces.

In the afternoon Ada would put on her bonnet, topshoes, and cloak and the two would wander together over the estate and sometimes over neighboring farms, bringing back pocketfuls of interesting leaves, seeds, insects, and stones. Ada would then arrange these finds into animal shapes on her table. She made a very good squirrel, all put together out of a week's collecting, that was so detailed that it had layer upon layer of tiny twigs for its fur.

On one of these walks Delwar was surprised but pleased when Ada took his hand. Perhaps if she had been of proper adult build for her sixteen years this affectionate gesture may have been confusing, but, as it stood, Delwar felt only great satisfaction, as if something in the spirit of his small, silent companion had seen into his soul and decided him good.

And so their lessons progressed. Ada gradually began to play in Delwar's presence, although for the first month she would play only when she thought he was out of hearing range. One day, she played a tune that she had learned by ear, a popular melody that her father often hummed. When she finished and turned away from the piano, she realized Delwar was standing in the doorway. He was smiling broadly and he raised his hands and clapped several times, but Ada was too modest to return his gaze. She left the piano and made as though to leave the room when Delwar said firmly, "All right. Today you will begin to learn to read music."

Learning to read music was a revelation to Ada. She had no idea that the written language of the piano could be so precise and complex. She loved to read books for the stories they told, the way a well-crafted tale could lead her to another life, worlds away from her own. And in reading music she found a similar transport, into another, new world with a new, beautiful language that in this household only she and Delwar could speak.

Once over her initial hesitation, Ada McGrath was a

good student of the piano. Delwar Haussler thought there might be nothing she could not achieve; he reflected warmly that she might one day be as accomplished as himself. In front of him she still played with a reticence born of shyness and reserve. However, this was not something that Delwar considered a flaw; he himself was a musician who valued formality and correctness over emoting and dramatic flourish.

Ada's piano lessons began to take precedence over her other pursuits, academic and domestic alike. They had never quite managed to commence the French tuition for which Delwar had also been engaged; once he had met Ada the young man felt embarrassed by the notion of imposing another language, a spoken one at that, on to his new pupil.

Wyston McGrath looked on with a slight unease; his daughter had always seemed possessed by the piano, and his idea of formal training had only served to accentuate the wild nature of her playing, despite adding structure and accuracy to her style. But these thoughts were easy for him to push to the back of his mind. After all, his only child's happiness mattered more than other considerations. Delwar Haussler had come with good references; the young man conformed to the household neatly. And Ada liked him.

$\mathcal{I}$T was not until several days after Ada made her expedition to the beach with Baines and Flora that Alisdair

Stewart returned from his property survey. He came through the bush still mounted on his horse, a large beast, no pony companion for Flora. The horse gingerly picked its way across the drying mud. Stewart surveyed the land around his house; he would have to organize another burning and clearing session. He was sure Ada would want to augment the vegetable patch, and he would have to find time to plant a lawn this year.

As he neared the house, Stewart could hear singing. It was a child's voice—Flora. The girl was singing, her thin young voice winding out to greet him, and the sound pleased Stewart, for it made him feel a homeliness he had not yet known in this place. He dismounted, trying to keep quiet. She sang a mournful tune, one he did not recognize. As he came through the door he realized that Flora was not unaccompanied. Ada sat at the kitchen table, her hands moving lightly across the wood, as though she were playing the keyboard of a phantom piano. "Hello," Stewart said softly. Ada and Flora immediately stopped their pantomime, both standing and moving away from the table. "Hello," responded Flora gaily, seeming almost surprised to see her stepfather return.

Uncomfortable under their gaze, the silence wide between them, Stewart took off his traveling hat, rubbed his unshaven chin, and went to the table, lifting the lace cloth from where Ada had replaced it. He ran his fingers over a pattern of etched grooves and marks; someone had carved a map of a piano keyboard into the tabletop. Shocked at this defacement of property, a table which he

himself had made, Alisdair Stewart concluded immediately that the carver must have been Ada; she had carved
it, now she played upon it. He lowered the cloth and
went back outside, a childlike disappointment fueling his
adult rage at being so depreciated by his new family.

Ada had not intended to anger her husband. She had
only been missing her piano, and had been pestered by a
restless Flora into their old routine of afternoon singing
lessons once the day's chores had been conquered. Flora
had insisted that the table was in fact a piano and that the
wooden keyboard sounded most lovely when played.
The child had taken a pencil to the table and drawn a
crude keyboard onto it and demanded that Ada play
when she herself grew tired of the toneless thumping of
fingers on wood. Ada, frustrated by the roughness of
Flora's approximation, had taken it upon herself to mark
out a correct keyboard with the kitchen knife, making
Flora name each key, "Middle C, C Sharp, D, D Sharp,
E, F, F Sharp . . ." and so on up the scale. Until Stewart
arrived home, it had not occurred to either that anything
might be amiss in this action.

But Stewart, unhappy at being reminded immediately
upon returning of his own insufficient efforts at helping
Ada and Flora feel more at home, began to worry about
Ada's carving. The markings grew in his mind until he
imagined them a sinister sign of something other.

Stewart paid a visit to his Aunt Morag at the mission
house the next day. The mission house was of more
sturdy and permanent structure than other buildings in

the area, with polished wooden stair banisters, heavy
wood paneling, lace curtains, wallpaper hung on all the
walls, and Morag's own samplers with biblical quotations
adorning the mantelpiece. Aunt Morag's parlor resem-
bled that of a Scottish house more fully than any other
home Stewart frequented. He found its comforts wel-
coming. Morag's mission girls, Heni and Mary, sewed
while Stewart helped his aunt to make angel wings for the
Christmas play.

Alisdair Stewart was not accustomed to being in the
company of Maori people, despite the fact that they had
helped in the construction of his house and in almost
every other endeavor he undertook in his homesteading.
Aunt Morag and Nessie, however, were devoted to the
Reverend's mission to bring Christianity to these heathen
people and lived comfortably among their converts, well
used to their manners and their habits, which, even when
altered by training, Alisdair found barbaric.

Heni and Mary were young stalwarts of the mission.
They dressed in a manner Stewart considered proper,
fully European. They were good seamstresses and Heni
had even become adept at helping Morag coax her hair
into the fine ringlets and tiny waxed loops that were her
only concession to vanity. They were well trained in polite domestic behavior, even though they constantly cor-
rupted themselves with their demonstrative displays of
affection toward each other, and with the clay tobacco
pipes to which they were addicted.

When Stewart came back inside after retrieving some

wood, George Baines followed behind. Baines was an in-frequent visitor at the mission house, normally coming only when there was business that needed tending; he could not abide by the social niceties observed by Stewart and the other settlers. Thus he made it his own rule to wait and take his tea in the kitchen.

Morag looked up from her sewing. She narrowed her eyes, examining her nephew Alisdair as he passed some handiwork to Nessie. "Well, you stopped combing your hair, which is a good thing, it was looking overdone," she said. Stewart reddened slightly. "You see," she continued, holding up the sheet on which she worked, "these are the slits that the heads will go through—show him, Nessie . . . In the play they'll be dead. The Reverend is going to use animal blood. No doubt it will be very dramatic."

". . . It will be very dramatic!" chimed Nessie.

Aunt Morag rounded on her companion. "Tea!" she commanded. As Nessie stood, Stewart leaned toward his aunt, his expression concerned, hesitant, "Aunt, what would you think if someone played a kitchen table like it were a piano?"

"Like it were a piano?" asked Morag, puzzled.

"It is strange, isn't it? I mean, it's not a piano, it doesn't make any sound."

Aunt Morag looked up at Nessie as she handed Stewart his tea. "Biscuits!" she hissed. She paused, then, "No, no sound," she confirmed.

"I knew she was mute," continued Stewart, "but now

I'm thinking perhaps it is more than that. I'm wondering if she's not brain-affected."

"No sound at all?" repeated the puzzled Morag.

"No, it was a table."

"Well, she was very violent with the gown. She tore off a chunk of lace. If I hadn't been there to see it, I'd have sworn she'd used her teeth"—at this point Nessie joined in and they spoke with simultaneous indignation—"and wiped her feet on it!"

"Well, it hasn't come to anything yet, just something of concern, that's all," Stewart said quickly.

George Baines stood in the dark doorway of the parlor, drinking his tea out of a fine china cup, incongruous in his rough hands. He listened to Stewart speak with a trace of amused interest in his eyes. Aunt Morag opened her fan and began to use it rapidly. "Oh yes, yes of course, just a concern," she said, her brow furrowing.

"There's something to be said for silence," continued Stewart, stirring his tea.

"Oh indeed," replied Morag, replacing her fan. "Cotton!" she demanded, holding up her needle for Nessie to thread.

Stewart began to sound relieved. "And with time, she will, I'm sure, become affectionate."

"Certainly," said Morag, "there is nothing so easy to like as a pet, and they are quite silent."

Baines listened without comment as he sipped his tea. He was not surprised to hear the table-piano story. He had witnessed Ada's communion with her piano, and now felt he had some understanding of her frustration at being kept from the object of her devotion.

After tea, Stewart and Baines walked the distance to Stewart's, where they found Flora riding an imaginary pony around the house. Stewart immediately commenced the daily chore of chopping wood. "The grand old Duke of York, he had ten thousand men . . ." sang Flora as she skipped, carrying logs back and forth between the woodpile and the chopping block, her white bonnet and starched pinafore crisp and pure against the black mud. Flora seized every opportunity to be in the open air when it was not raining, and she liked to help Stewart with his work. She enjoyed rooting in the vegetable patch and chasing the chickens and had begun to explore the bush nearest the house, the dark undergrowth appealing to her keen sense of adventure. She flinched each time Stewart's axe struck the woodchop, but continued with her task happily. Baines began to talk.

"Those eighty acres, that cross the stream, what do you think of them?"

"On your property?"

"Yes," Baines replied as he took a log to Stewart, who talked without pausing in his work.

"Good flattish land with reliable water—why? I don't have any money, what are you on about?" asked Stewart.

"I'd like to make a swap," replied Baines.

"What for?"

"The piano." Baines picked up another log.

"The piano on the beach?" Stewart asked, as though there might be another. He stopped working, this matter required serious attention. Baines nodded. "It's not marshy, is it?" he asked, immediately suspicious.

"No," Baines laughed.

Stewart swung the axe down onto the chopping block and crossed his arms, smiling broadly, very pleased with this deal. "Well, Baines the music lover, I never would have thought. Hidden talents, George."

Baines laughed again. "I'd have to get lessons," he said, smiling. "It wouldn't be much use without them."

"Yes, I suppose you would." Stewart looked down at the ground and then back at Baines, calculating. "Well, Ada can play." Baines shrugged, remaining silent. "I have it in a letter she plays well. She's been playing since she was five or six." Stewart appeared to take strange pride in his wife's achievement, despite the fact he did not want her to have the piano. For his part Baines did not indicate that he already knew how well Ada could play.

"*W*HAT on?" Flora asked, prompted by Ada. Stewart had just told of his trade for land with Baines and he was flushed with excitement over his plans. They were all seated at the kitchen table having had a simple meal that Ada had prepared carefully. She could not cook well, nor was she accomplished at the other domestic duties expected of her, but she was too proud to admit either inexperience or difficulty. Flora, having poured three cups

from her own miniature china tea set, was drinking tea
with the adults, her mother and the man that she still
looked upon as "stepfather," a notion as abstract as the
idea of "New Zealand" had been.

"On your piano," Stewart told Ada, "that is the swap."

Ada signed to Flora, her black eyes large with sudden
fury.

"What does she say?" asked Stewart, frustrated once
more by the indirect nature of their communication, and
taken aback by his wife's emotional response to his news.

"She says it's her piano, and she won't have him touch
it," Flora interpreted, her voice infused with her mother's
indignation. Ada stood and walked back and forth, agitated, ire mounting inside her. She paused to signal rapidly. "He's an oaf, he can't read, he's ignorant." Ada
began to kick at the furniture, stamping her feet with singular force, no longer able to conceal her rage.

"He wants to improve himself . . ." Stewart began with
growing impatience. At that, Ada smashed a teacup to
the floor, china fragments scattering beneath her feet.
". . . And you'll be able to play it."

Ada knew then that Stewart had no inkling of how she
felt. Burning with anger, she began to pull his freshly
laundered shirts down from the line above the wood-
stove, flinging them to the floor. Then she opened her
notepad and began to write furiously, her hand shaking
as she clutched the silver pencil.

"Teach him how to look after it," said Stewart, his
voice harsh.

Ada handed him the note that read, "NO, NO, THE PIANO IS MINE. IT'S MINE."

Appalled and angered by this display of emotion and obduracy, Stewart slammed the note, and his fist, onto the table, upsetting the rest of the cups. He stood. "You can't go on like this. We're a family now, we all make sacrifices and so will you," he shouted, pointing at Ada violently. "You will teach him. And I will see to it." He turned and walked stiffly outside, leaving Ada suddenly pale and still, her eyes fixed on the door that Stewart had just slammed. Accustomed as she was to being indulged, her will never transgressed, Stewart's behavior, from the moment she had arrived, seemed inexplicable and hard. There was nothing he could have done to hurt her more. But deep down Ada knew she had no choice, and this as much as anything outraged her nature. She angrily resolved to do her husband's bidding, in the most minimal terms, and if Mr. Baines should begin to regret his purchase and find his lessons grim, well, so be it, yes good.

Stewart paced the mud in front of the house, still pulsing with anger. His ordered life had been turned upside down; nothing was proceeding as he had hoped it might.

ALISDAIR STEWART had emigrated to New Zealand when he was a young man of twenty. He had come intending to farm, with great plans of house-building and livestock-keeping. The grueling length of the journey had not dampened his enthusiasm—nor had the tropical in-

tensity of the bush where he hoped to amass a great farming estate. Stewart left behind in Scotland one brother,
Thomas, and an elderly mother who was perennially un-
well.

"Not enough land, not enough work for two men,
Alisdair," Thomas had said one day; Alisdair knew that
his elder brother had marriage plans and that the farm
was not large enough for two families. Scotland was a
land of emigration, generation after generation had left
and were still leaving. It was then that he decided he too
would leave. It was only a question of when and on which
distant shore he should set his sights.

Although he did not discuss it with anyone, Thomas
included, Alisdair Stewart entertained his own hopes of
marriage. He was naturally far from impetuous and knew
anyway that it was important to be sensible about such
things, and to plan carefully. Louisa Douglas, a girl from
a good family in the village, caught his eye; she was fair-
haired, blue-eyed, and tall, as tall as Alisdair himself at
fourteen, although his growth had surpassed hers in recent years. Alisdair had walked Louisa home to her farm
after church on two or three occasions, but the time
could not be spared often. Still, walking with Louisa had
inspired Alisdair, and although he had seen her but once
during these past few months, his thoughts returned to
her frequently.

The young man settled on New Zealand: There was
land for inexpensive purchase, passage was available from
Glasgow, and a spirit of adventure was attached to emi-

grations of distance this great. Alisdair's sights had not extended as far as the Antipodes, but he knew that there the seasons progressed on an opposite time scale, so that Christmas and Hogmanay took place during summer. The minister from the kirk told him that there were many good Scottish Presbyterians in New Zealand, and this led Alisdair to imagine villages with churches, farms, fields, and houses not very different, apart from the up- side-down seasons, from home. Not long after having made his decision, a letter arrived from their father's sis- ter, Aunt Morag; she herself was traveling that very week to New Zealand on a mission with her young companion and funds raised by their church. "They say that land is plentiful and there is bounty," wrote Aunt Morag, "and a great many heathen souls to be saved." Alisdair felt all the signs for his own journey were fortuitous.

Another piece of land was sold. Two packing crates were filled with possessions, his clothes, his few books— the Bible, Shakespeare, Defoe's *Robinson Crusoe*. This would be enough, along with the money, to help him build his first home. At night Alisdair lay awake chilled to the marrow with excitement and apprehension.

And Louisa Douglas, Alisdair wondered, when would she join him? Immediately, or after enough time had elapsed to build a house? One month before his depar- ture, Alisdair managed to secure a Sunday when he could accompany Louisa home from church. It was a fine spring day, and all of God's creatures seemed to be shak- ing off the dull, gray winter. Over the hills Alisdair talked and talked, telling Louisa all his plans down to the last detail, including each item wrapped securely in his packing crate. He thought that by talking he might enthuse her; she nodded and listened attentively. She knew a little more of New Zealand than did Alisdair himself. "It is a land of savages," she offered, "a land of hot springs and cannibals."

Cannibals, thought Alisdair, his New Zealand dreamland of Scottish churches, farms, and fields flickering and, for a moment, being replaced by Crusoe and lone footprints on the beach. "Well," he replied, "Aunt Morag has gone on a mission. By the time I arrive, the savages will be Christians, and they'll all be having scones with their tea." They laughed and, too soon, they arrived at Louisa's home.

"Good-bye, Alisdair Stewart," said Louisa, and he thought he could hear rue in her tone.

"Good-bye, Miss Douglas," he replied, lowering his hat in his hands, smiling awkwardly. He did not ask, "And will you follow me, will we marry, will you be my wife and travel after me?" He did not say, "Wait, and I'll send for you, and you will come to the new land and bring your dresses and your hymnbook and your fine Scottish ways." These were his thoughts, but being young and shy and unrefined in the ways of seduction, all he said was, "I will write you letters." This seemed to him romance in all its splendor.

And so he traveled on a ship whose cargo held the packing-crate possessions and dreams of other settlers like himself, hopeful young men and a handful of women who were leaving, in some cases escaping, the old world, in search of the new. They took an eccentric array of things with them, iron bedsteads, china cabinets, and dining room tables taken in advance of any parlor, kitchen, or bedroom to receive them.

And on his great journey Alisdair Stewart dreamed of Louisa, her hair blowing in the ship's breeze. He dreamed of cannibals also, large people with red teeth. They threatened Louisa Douglas but Alisdair saved her from their knives and gaping mouths over and over again.

Alisdair Stewart arrived at New Zealand and was impressed by the steamy nature of the heat. He transported his packing crates inland to the locale of his land claim. There was nothing there; there was everything there, more trees, more wild, brilliant many-hued plants—more growth—than he had ever seen in the gardens and bare hills of Scotland. He built a kind of lean-to under which he could sleep and store his things out of the rain, although the creeping damp of the wet forest seeped into everything. And then he began to work, cutting, burning, and building. There was no time for letter writing although at night he still dreamed of Louisa Douglas.

After four months during which he saw no one except the Maoris who lived in the area, a strange people, he decided, although they seemed tame enough, hardly cannibals, Alisdair Stewart traveled on horseback to Stratford for supplies. There he found three letters waiting for him: one from his brother Thomas containing a banker's

draft and a few words from the farm that made Alisdair
nearly ill with homesickness; one from Aunt Morag announcing that she had decided to come south to live at
the mission nearest Alisdair; and one from his sister
Mary with news of the birth of her first child and all the
village gossip she thought might interest her brother, including the news, passed very casually, that Louisa Douglas was to wed the following spring. The map on the wall
of the general office showed that Alisdair Stewart was in a
country at the bottom of world. Louisa Douglas could
not be farther away.

𝒜DA MᴄGRATH's piano had to be traded. Stewart
had sent for a wife, a helpmeet, someone to assuage the
loneliness he was beginning to feel in middle age and that
he knew would worsen with time. He had not bargained
for a wife who would hold a box of wood and ivory more
dear than the wishes of her own husband.

Stewart believed that his survival depended upon the
acquisition of land. Farming was difficult and slow; land
was his only real currency. There was no time for leisure,
for the luxurious pursuits of distant cities and salons; if
Ada McGrath was so devoted to music, she could volun-
teer to play the mission hall piano. To Alisdair Stewart
land was infinitely more important than the piano on the
beach, but what truly pleased him was the unexpected
good use he had finally made of her piano; eighty acres
was a very good trade.

Chapter *5*

AND so it was that George Baines traveled once again to the beach for the piano. This time he was accompanied not by one small woman and her daughter but by a party of eight Maori men, Chief Nihe's son Hone included. George Baines had become proficient in the Maori language and had adopted some of their ways, ways that he found natural and sympathetic to his New Zealand bush life. When he needed to barter labor there were always men willing to help him; Baines found these negotiations much simpler than Alisdair Stewart who, with his proud, pious certainties, was the object of unconverted Maori scorn.

The piano remained where they had left it marooned like the wreck of a ship on the beach. Since Ada's pilgrimage it had not been without visitors. There were footprints on the sand surrounding the crate, and some of the boards had been pulled back where Baines had replaced them. Thinking of the way that Ada McGrath had played renewed Baines' enthusiasm for possessing the thing, enthusiasm now much needed as the instrument could not have been more awkward to transport along the narrow footpaths through the mist-laden trees. The men struggled, grunting and swearing.

"*Hiki na ake muri na!*—Lift up the back!" Hone commanded.

"*Tero*—*tero!*—arsehole!" came the blunt reply.

"*Hei niti niti maau!*—You lick it!" There was much laughter, and Baines turned from his task of path clearing to join in. At that moment, someone stumbled and the back of the piano crashed to the ground, thundering out in the bottom end of the scale, the sound carrying across a great sweep of bush. The men scattered, as though the beast within the crate had risen to life.

Once the piano came to rest in Baines' hut, the men all strewn across the floor and porch, resting, George Baines removed the crating. The piano was revealed to him as a thing of unusual beauty; despite its recent maltreatment, there was a sheen discernible beneath the layer of salt that had crept over the rosewood. Baines set to cleaning the instrument, starting on the legs that had been exposed to the greatest abuse from the sea. He worked upwards, cleaning and oiling, restoring some of the piano's dignity. When he reached the ivory keys he thought to polish them with a drop of wax. As he rubbed, the notes sounded beneath his fingers and even his untutored ear could detect a slackness, an atonal vibration, to the strings.

ADA MCGRATH mounted her husband's horse and was led by Alisdair Stewart along the path to George Baines' hut. Flora perched in front of Ada, pleased to be upon a horse, but even the warmth of her daughter's body did not lift Ada's spirits. The path sloped up through a strange, bearded forest, where the tops of the trees were bare and glittering; each time she entered this landscape, Ada thought it alien in some new and perplexing way, as though the land itself changed shape nightly.

"I'd try children's tunes," Stewart advised, "nothing more complicated . . ." He glanced up at his wife on the horse, but Ada would not look at him. She might be obedient, but she was unrepentant, and she did not want to teach the piano to its new owner, George Baines.

"Just be encouraging, no one expects him to be good," Stewart said, again looking back at Ada. His wife's face remained closed, unmoving.

On their arrival, Baines greeted the threesome politely, smiling shyly in the direction of the women who made no attempt to acknowledge him. Inside, the rosy wood of the piano shone out of place, the only polished furniture in the rough hut. Alisdair Stewart walked over to the instrument, running his hand along the top, and then lifted the lid, at last curious about the object he had traded away. "It looks good," he said smiling and nodding at Ada. "Very nice-looking thing. Well . . ." he turned to Baines, who also smiled openly, expecting Ada to be pleased that he had retrieved the piano from the torment of the sea. "I wish you luck," said Stewart. "The girls are very excited about the lessons."

Ada and Flora McGrath looked anything but excited; Flora, shy and not unaware of the tension emanating from her mother, tugged obsessively at a long strand of hair that had broken free of her bonnet. Ada stared firmly at the floor, cold and grim.

"Flora will explain anything Ada says," Stewart said lightly. "They talk through their fingers. You can't believe what they say with just their hands." With that Stewart bade his farewell, abandoning his wife and her child to their piano lesson.

George Baines walked toward the piano. He lifted the lid, admiring the gloss of the keys, wanting to show Ada that the lessons might begin. Ada signed to Flora, and Flora spoke to Baines: "My mother wants to see your hands. Hold them out."

Baines hesitated, then held out his hands, spread wide as if holding a globe.

"No, no, like this . . ." Flora brought her own neat little fingers together, first with their backs up, then turning them over. Baines, shyly keen, did the same, only his hands were big and coarse and spoke of his life.

Ada signed to Flora: "You have to wash them."

"They are washed."

"Wash them again."

Baines looked down at his hands as though they belonged to a stranger. "The marks do not come off," he said slowly, offering them for Ada's inspection. Ada looked away. "These are scars and hardened skin."

Ada and Flora did not move, although the child stared at Baines' scabrous hands, fascinated. Baines, his shoulders heavy, took a tin bucket down from where it hung on the wall, dropping a scrubbing brush and soap into it with a dull clank. Ada watched through the small window as Flora, standing beside Baines, gravely indicated where he should scrub.

Furtively, Ada moved to her piano. She longed to touch it, but she was torn by her affections, wanting the sensation of the ivory keys beneath her fingers, but knowing it was no longer hers to touch. She felt as though the piano had become a forbidden thing. She stroked the varnished wood, her hand barely glancing the surface, then softly lifted the lid. One hand to her mouth as though to steel herself, she laid a finger on a key, pressing the ivory downward very slowly. A muffled note sounded, and Ada gently played a few more, then suddenly drew back. The instrument was horribly out of tune, every note warped and hollowed beyond recognition. Snapping down the lid, Ada went outside where Flora was still watching over Baines. Ada signed abruptly, making her way down the steps of the veranda.

"There's no tune left in the piano," Flora said, "so she can't teach you."

*T*HE PIANO tuner was blind and it was arduous to transport him from Otaki; he had to be carried on Baines' back for much of the way. Baines took pleasure in watching the white-haired old man touch the piano, listening as its health was restored.

"Ah, a. . . Broadwood," said the tuner as he ran his seeing hands over the wood. "A fine instrument. I've not seen one here, nor in New South Wales where I have tuned some two hundred. Yes, they like their pianos there." Out of his pocket he took a carefully wrapped tuning fork. He uncovered the fork, lifted the back and lid of the piano and began to tune, drawing the strings taut as they criss-crossed in the manner of all boxed grands. Leaning close to the instrument he sniffed the air. Baines watched as the piano tuner put his nose to the keys. "Scent," he said. "And salt, of course."

"What will you play when it's tuned?"

"I can't play," said Baines.

"You don't play?" The blind old tuner straightened up, stunned, and then slowly he began to laugh. The enormous futility of their long bush journey into this remote valley at first seemed tragic, but this man's simple admission struck him more sweetly, such that their adventure together had all the best qualities of divine farce.

"Well, my dear Miss Broadwood," he said, patting the piano on its lid, "tuned but silent." The tuner continued, shaking his head and chuckling. "Perhaps I understand you better than you know. My wife, you see, sang with a bell-clear tone. After we married she stopped. She said she didn't feel like singing, that life made her sad. And that's how she lived, lips clamped over a perfect voice."

But George Baines had not traded land and transported the piano to his hut as an object to be merely looked upon in silence; he knew that, with it in tune, Ada McGrath would be unable to resist the instrument. He began to anticipate his next lesson and the opportunity, once again, to be in the presence of Ada McGrath and her uncanny music, which had resonated in his thoughts and dreams since the day at the beach.

$\mathcal{A}$D A lay awake at night, not dreaming, not sleeping. She felt a queer mixture of churning emotion. She was relieved that the piano had been rescued from where it sat, sinking into the sand, yet she could not believe that Alisdair Stewart had bargained away the only possession for which she cared, the only thing save her daughter that gave her pleasure and freedom in life. She would not have traveled all this way to lose her piano. It was as though Stewart had deprived her of her voice, voiceless as she remained. Her loss was the pain of losing one's love, and she was bereft, her heart broken. The piano was the only thing she had ever been encouraged to master, to make her own, and thinking of it in this manner led her thoughts to Delwar Haussler. Abruptly, she put that memory away and turned over in the small bed she shared with Flora.

$\mathcal{T}$H E day of the next lesson soon arrived. Ada dressed slowly that morning; the layers and layers of clothes felt heavy, the pantaloons, the hoops, petticoats, bodice, chemise, stays. She had brought from Scotland a sturdy wardrobe all made of good and pretty cloth, striped dark tartans in purple, black, and blue, plain high-collared working dresses, as well as one or two favorite silks; but already the New Zealand clime had placed a wearing strain on these garments. The mud, the damp warmth seemed impossible to rinse away in the primitive tub and washbasin to which she sometimes felt she had been chained. It was not just her own clothes, and Flora's, that needed to be kept clean, but—along with the cooking and floor-scrubbing—Alisdair Stewart's as well, and his were especially difficult to wash. Every time Stewart entered her bedroom he seemed to knock the hoops from their hanging place on the wall. And there he was to fetch them now, to send Ada and her daughter on their way to George Baines.

Halfway along the path to Baines' hut, Ada was overcome by a sudden longing. She sat down on the mossy, fern-mantled ground, spreading her dark cloak beneath her deep red dress. Flora sprawled behind her, eyes closed, feeling the warm sun pass over her face, the straw bonnet she wore catching the light and holding it there. Tuned as she was to her mother's emotions, Flora found herself thinking of Scotland, of her pony Gabriel, and the roller skates she had left behind. She played with a bit of fern plucked from the earth while her mother sat upright, overwhelmed by a fervid homesickness, the strength of which near made her faint. What was her father doing now, was he thinking of her? Would she ever see him again? How were the seasons passing in Aberdeen? Why had she agreed to travel so far away? Ada longed to return to the familiar rooms and corridors of the house in which she had always lived. She had not known that separation from her home would be so painful, she could not have guessed. And what was this place where she found herself now, what kind of life could she live here?

After a spell during which Ada struggled to cast off her despair, she rose, alerted Flora, and they continued on their way. At the end of the path Ada sent her daughter ahead to knock on the door of Baines' hut. She waited at a distance while Flora relayed what she had been told to say. "Mother says she can't stand to teach piano with it all out of tune. So I'm to do scales." Flora entered the dark hut while Ada continued to wait outside, beyond the porch. She sat down at the piano and, turning to George Baines, spoke in a manner she thought might be teacherly, "I hope you've scrubbed your hands." She commenced to play, stopping almost immediately. "Oh, it's in tune," she commented, surprised. She then began a scale more confidently.

At the sound of the piano, clear and precise, Ada McGrath came forward, entering the hut. She hastened to the instrument and sat next to Flora, moving the child out of the way. She placed her hands on the keys and played a few chords, unable to believe what she heard. The tone was good, the notes sounded exact, mathemati-

cal even. Ada continued to play chords while Flora ob-
jected. "I'm teaching him," she said, unwilling to relin-
quish her position, but Ada ignored the child and Flora
stumped away. She played another chord and then
looked up at George Baines who smiled with pleasure at
her surprise. Ada stood and walked away from the piano,
signing to Flora. "Mother would like to see what you can
play."

"I'd rather not play," Baines said hesitantly. "I want to
listen and learn that way."

Flora and Ada both frowned. "Everyone has to practice," said Flora bossily. She had been made to practice
enough herself.

"I just want to listen," Baines insisted in his plain way.

Ada felt nonplussed. She did not want to have an audience any more than she wanted to teach. But, feeling
obliged by her husband's cold bargain, obliged in the end
to her father in Scotland and the bargain for her hand
which he had made, she went forward to the piano. She
opened the lid abruptly, trapping Baines' finger where he
leaned against the instrument casually. He snatched his
hand away—she made no show of apology. She played a
short simple scale and looked up at the man who had
purchased her piano away from her, as if to say, "Well,
you have listened. There, is that enough?"

"Lovely," said George Baines, by way of encouragement.

And so, slowly, belligerently, Ada began to play. She
would fulfill her husband's trading pact, however reluc-

tantly. And yet, before she knew what was happening, her anger faded and her absorption in the music grew. Almost immediately, the music took her away from this dirty, crude hut with its open, smoking fire, the stale loaf of bread left out on the table, and this man who could not read or play; away from all the difficulties of her new life. Baines stood listening by the window, while Flora, still disappointed that she was no longer Baines' teacher herself, wandered outside. Ada played for one hour before she grew weary of the gaze of George Baines, which she felt burn into her back. As if he could learn by staring!

*T*HAT evening Ada was despondent. She felt a loneliness as deep and dark as the sea. There was so much work to be done in this place, she could see it would never cease. The reduction in her father's circumstances as he grew older and let the estate run down had forced Ada to take on an increased share of the domestic labor. But the labor of her father's house was nothing compared to the work of every day here in her husband's home, where there was nothing to add levity to her tasks. Ada did not object to the work, it was a way of passing time, a way of filling the hours during which she would have played music had she been at home with her piano. But it never seemed to end, this toil, and at night Ada went to bed heavy with fatigue.

Alisdair Stewart was away working on his property often; his nights were sometimes spent camping on some corner of the patchwork of bush he saw as his estate. And when he was in the house, he kept distance between himself and his wife. After the outburst over the piano, they had both become very polite and stubborn with one another, Stewart's commonplaces tinged with guilt, Ada's countenance cool and distant.

On this night, Alisdair was home and reading in the next room when Ada tucked Flora into bed. Flora wanted to be told a story, she wanted to be told about her father. "I've told you the story of your father many, many times," signed Ada, smiling. Flora never grew tired of hearing about her father. Ada herself did not really tire of the telling, even though after these years and for a complex web of reasoning, Ada had not yet told Flora the complete story, but only a few simple and reassuring versions of the truth.

"Oh, tell me again," insisted Flora, reaching up to caress her mother's face, drawing her near in the warm, golden light of the candlelamp. "Was he a teacher?" Ada nodded. "How did you speak to him?"

"I didn't need to speak," Ada signed. "I could lay thoughts out in his mind like they were a sheet." Her hands smoothed the air.

"What happened? Why didn't you get married?" Flora asked, her brow furrowing as it always did at this moment in the story.

"He became frightened and stopped listening," Ada replied.

Just then Alisdair Stewart opened the door of the

room. He stopped, as though prevented from entering by an invisible barrier. "Shall I kiss you good-night?" he asked Flora, although Ada felt the question directed at herself. Flora slid down beneath the blanket; she did not want Stewart to come near. Ada remained expressionless. Alisdair nodded, then he turned and left the room heavily, closing the door.

$\mathcal{F}$LORA and Ada made the walk to George Baines' hut for the next piano lesson through the endless rain. Baines kept a friendly mongrel dog whom he called Flynn, and Flora's pleasure was to torment Flynn with a stick. The dog complied with her games passively, taking refuge under the hut when her enthusiasm grew too great, whereupon Flora tried to force him out into the driving rain by pushing her weapon through a hole in the veranda floor, her excited leaping and shouting keeping tempo with her mother's rhythmic melodies.

Inside, George Baines paced the floor of his hut while Ada McGrath played in her insatiable manner, the music at once lyrical and insistent. She had dropped all efforts to teach Baines, and now played for her own pleasure, stealing time for herself from beneath his gaze.

Baines had heard singers and players in the drinking houses of many ports; he had sung sailor's tunes himself at sea; he had stamped his feet and danced with women who lifted their skirts and whirled gaily. It was nothing like this. His listening was not refined, nor discerning, and yet Ada McGrath's playing made him hear, made his mind open and fill with emotion. He felt he could listen to her play forever. He observed that she played a steady rhythm with her left hand, and a counterrhythm with her right. One piece seemed to flow into the next without cessation. These were not parlor songs, or jigs, or popular tunes; they were harmonies from somewhere else. Baines was drawn to Ada, to her self-contained silence at the keys. It was as though the music brought this silence strangely alive.

Baines kept his head bowed, but as the playing became more confident and she became more absorbed, he raised his eyes to watch. He sat at a far corner of the room, enjoying the whole vision of this woman at her piano.

Presently Baines took his chair to a closer position and opposite angle. Ada glanced up as she felt him passing behind her. She thought it odd that he always seemed satisfied to listen, not wanting to play was beyond her imagining. She became engrossed in the music once again while his attention focused on her as she bent farther from or closer to the keys.

Again Baines shifted his chair, carrying it round the back and to the other side of the piano. Ada watched him as he moved, conscious of his scrutiny, the shifting heat of his presence. From this position Baines could see more clearly and thus enjoy her fingers moving fluidly on the keys and the small details of emotion on her face. Her hands were so very supple, her fingers tapered, strong but delicate and fine. Twice he closed his eyes and breathed deeply, suffused with longing and appetence. When his eyes were closed, Ada glanced at him warily.

While George Baines listened, he thought of the sea, he thought of his own travels. In his mind, women and music went together. And this woman, with her slender expressive back and her small hands that yet could reach so far across the keys, played as though she was transported, as lost in her piano music here in his hut as she had been on the beach. She had fashioned her hair differently today, Baines observed, thin elaborate plaits that curled around her ears and left her neck quite bare. Baines stared hard. Her long white neck, still damp from the rain through which she had walked, was irresistible. Without thinking of what he was doing, he crossed the room, placed one hand on her shoulder, leaned down and kissed the perfect nape of her neck.

Gasping, Ada leapt away from the piano, her hand covering her mouth as though to suppress a cry. She went toward the door unsteadily. "Ada," said Baines, conscious that he had made a grave mistake. "Wait . . . wait." He spoke quickly and quietly, not thinking of what he would say, not wanting her to leave. "Do you know how . . . to bargain?" The proposition came to his mind out of nowhere, fully formulated.

Ada turned and looked at George Baines, her face tense and leery.

"There's a way you can have your piano back." George Baines had not planned this, but he found himself speaking as though he had. "Do you want it back?" he asked quietly, knowing how she would reply.

Ada would not meet his gaze.

"Do you want it back?" he asked more loudly.

Ada's eyes met his. She looked at him steadily, waiting for him to speak.

"You see, I'd like us to make a deal." George Baines looked away. Having gone this far, he might well continue. "There's things I'd like to do while you play."

Ada drew her breath with quick disgust. He was as crude as he appeared. She turned to gather her sheets of music, her cloak and bonnet.

"If you let me you can earn it back," he offered.

She stepped toward the door.

"What do you think? One visit for every key."

Ada paused. She looked at the piano. If she left now she would never see it again. She paced slowly around the back of the Broadwood, which had always been part of her life, part of her very soul, her face reflected in the polished surface of the rosewood. George Baines waited. She paused a long while, her mind racing, at the far side of the instrument, before finally clearing her throat as though to speak. She held up one finger and then pointed to her shoulder.

"Your dress?" asked Baines. Ada shook her head and bunched the cloth of her skirt in her fist.

"Skirt . . . ?" Frustrated by his lack of understanding, she ran her finger back and forth over the black keys of the piano. "For every black one?" asked Baines. "That's a lot less. Half," he said, still bargaining. Ada started for the door again. "All right," he conceded, moving to one side to intercept her, "all right then, the black keys."

Ada gathered her skirts gracefully and sat back down at the piano. She had succeeded in reducing her payment to half and felt, even within these compromising circumstances, proud. She played the lowest black key, held one finger in the air, and then began to play.

$\mathscr{B}$EFORE he built his hut in the bush, George Baines lived his life on the sea. He was born in a village on the northeast coast of England, outside Hull, in a community that fished for its livelihood. George grew up on boats, he knew the sea through the bottom of his boat like some men know land through riding horseback over it. Yet by the time he was sixteen George Baines had tired of the endless grueling seasons of his father's trade; he wanted something bigger, grander, and he soon knew how that ambition might be fulfilled. He had heard talk in a public house full of drunken sailors whose stories got bigger as the evening wore away.

Whales. The great, burly, air-blowing fish of the sea. George Baines had seen a gray whale once, when he was twelve and accompanying his father in the boat on his own for the first time. George had been taking a moment's relaxation, lying back in the sun, sipping his father's strong-brewed coffee, when suddenly the calm water fifty feet off starboard surged, and a great gray back broke the surface, shattering George's daydream. He sat up, knocking his coffee mug into the sea. He cried out, and his father, thinking his son in peril, stood from where he was working in the back of the boat in time to see the whale spout. A plume of spray flew high into the air, and one of the things George Baines remembered most clearly was the foul stench that came with it as the droplets settled in their direction. The whale broke the water's surface once again, bringing even more of its great bulk out of the ocean before it sank back down, not to reappear.

For George Baines the sighting of this whale provided a kind of epiphany. It impressed upon him, yet again, the surly power of the sea. In his village, most fishing seasons took casualties, the lives of men young and strong, and George Baines had never thought the ocean that provided his family's livelihood benevolent. But the appearance of the whale both astonished and made the boy of twelve years afraid.

Baines did become a whaler, and he did travel the oceans for many years in search of the sperm whale, the unaccompanied, secluded white whale, and to more southern latitudes in pursuit of the right whale. He returned home twice, once after six months, and then again after ten years when it took his father several moments to recognize his son's wind-rushed face. Baines grew accustomed to life on the sea. He liked the men with whom he worked, and he looked forward to the company of women in the ports. He loved the whales. He loved them as they died, as they were flayed at sea for oil and bones

and ambergris. But he grew tired of the slaughter, he grew
restless with his own restlessness, and one day at the
seething port of Hull he married a girl he had known
over the years. He took her from the bawdy house where
she lived, and they set up housekeeping in rooms over-
looking the high street, his savings in the bank, and a new
job in the port, on land, not on the ocean. They lived like
this for one year, and they were happy after a fashion.
Elizabeth couldn't cook, or sew, or do much at all except
have a good time, and so they did. But George grew
bored, and Elizabeth too, and they came to feel their life
was a kind of playacting. So George returned to the sea,
and Elizabeth to her old ways, and they parted amicably.
He gave her some money to get her started, and then he
booked his passage to the South Seas, heading for New
Zealand.

On this journey when his ship sighted whales, around
the Horn of Africa and in the waters surrounding his
destination, George watched the beasts rise from the
waves and felt pleased that he was bound for landfall, not
a bloody killing on the sea.

OUTSIDE George Baines' hut, huddled under the eaves
of the house, Flora now cradled Flynn the dog whom she
had wrapped in her red cloak. She stroked his ears and
his long nose and spoke to him. "Poor baby," she cooed.
"What horrid little person put you in the rain and shoved
you with a stick? Huh? Huh? You're all right with me."

She kissed the top of his head. When Flora accompanied Ada to the piano lessons she felt small anger each time her mother insisted she stay outside on her own. Flynn was her friend, her only friend, she thought with a degree of morbid pleasure. "We're all alone here," she whispered to the dog, "nobody loves you but me."

*A*s Ada picked her way back through the trees, Flora skipping happily alongside, she wondered what manner of bargain she had made, with what manner of man. But Ada, firm and resolute as she was, unassailable within her modest frame, did not think about the nature of her bargain for long: She had to keep it. She had to have her piano.

Chapter 6

PREPARATIONS for the Christmas play, a momentous event in the mission community's calendar, were under way. The Reverend Septimus Campbell, happily freed from the narrow gray prejudices of his native church, liked to blend the traditional children's Nativity play with something altogether more unconventional. He spent much of the year planning it, and for the few months leading up to the date the mission house was a blur of dramatic activity.

On this dark afternoon, Stewart was helping Aunt Morag fashion wands with painted moons and stars dangling from one end, while the Reverend was busy cutting shapes from cardboard. "Scissors," Aunt Morag demanded imperiously of her nephew, like a surgeon giving orders to a nurse. Stewart passed the wicker sewing basket to her.

"Nessie," said the Reverend, "put that down, and come and put your hand out." Nessie, about to serve tea, was carrying a tray loaded with teacups, sweet biscuits, and cakes.

"Oh no. Use Mr. Stewart," she said, coyly, holding her head to one side.

"No, no, Nessie please," said the Reverend. But when Nessie turned away, the Reverend, anxious to get on with his work, decided to enlist the help of Mary, one of the Maori girls. "Kneel down here," he pointed. Mary moved across obediently.

Horrified at the thought of being upstaged, Nessie quickly put down her tray. "Oh, all right then," she said, with a girlish shake of her head, crouching where the Reverend had indicated.

"Put out your hand, then," said the Reverend, who was wearing a tiny pair of angel wings. Nessie held her hand up, basking in the attention of all present, but when the Reverend raised the cardboard axe above his head as though to strike her, she gasped and snatched her hand away. "No, no," said the Reverend impatiently. "Put out your hand, here." He raised his axe and brought it down with a flourish, narrowly missing Nessie. "Look, look, you are being attacked," he explained, positioning her hand again. This time, in the shadow cast on the wall, Nessie saw the axe coming down and chopping off her hand, the Reverend an axe-murderer, she his helpless victim. She gave a little squeal as the Reverend brought his axe down once more. The others laughed. "And with the blood," said the Reverend, "it will be a very good effect."

The Reverend's shadow stroked the cardboard axe

shadow meditatively, reveling in the brilliance of his dramatic devices, but his stroking of the axe caused Morag to shudder. Her brother's image on the parlor wall was menacing. The axe looked too real, and she wondered aloud if they were not going too far by having animal blood.

𝒯HE piano lessons took place once every three days, which was as much time as Ada could spare from the work of the house, although had the piano been her own she would doubtless have contrived to spend some hours every day escaping from domestic captivity. As was their habit, Flora accompanied her mother to George Baines' hut, but was made to remain outside during the lessons. When the dog Flynn heard Ada and Flora approaching, the swish of their skirts, Flora chattering, he ran to hide under the house. Flora wrapped her red cloak around herself, laid on her stomach under the veranda, and called to the dog. George Baines' hut was built on short stilts, to keep the wooden floor dry and free of vermin and insects. Flora crawled under a little way, but when it grew dark and musty and the sound of footsteps overhead frightened her, she backed out. "Flynn," she called, "Flynn," her frustration with the animal increasing. The dog, sensibly, remained well hidden.

Dismayed by the prospect of another afternoon alone, Flora climbed onto the veranda and knocked at the front door. "I want to speak to my mother," she demanded when Baines answered. Ada stopped playing and came onto the porch, closing the door behind her. "I don't want to be outside, I want to watch," insisted Flora.

"No," Ada signed, "you must calm down and play outside."

"I'll be very quiet."

"He's very shy and a beginner."

"I won't look at him," Flora pleaded. But Ada shook her head, determined to continue with the lesson. She was uncertain of Baines, of the terms of the bargain; Flora must stay outside. Ada disappeared into the hut, closing the door to her daughter once more. The little girl walked along the veranda slowly, her shoulders and chin low, disappointment and annoyance writ large on her face, while her mother's piano playing rippled from within. She bumped herself down onto the coarse bench. Unaccustomed to spending so much time on her own, and not used to her mother's attention being directed to anyone other than herself, Flora was not happy.

Inside, George Baines watched while Ada McGrath played her piano. Today her demeanor was different, more confident, more as it had been on the beach. He listened intently, his mind full, slaked, and still he wanted more. He paced the floor of his hut, circling ever closer, as an animal draws near to its prey. Ada played with her customary involvement, and yet she was aware of Baines' movements. When he stood, leaning over the back of the piano, his gaze fixed upon her, she looked up at him and then closed her eyes, wanting to be inside the music, no-where else.

𝒯HAT night, George Baines dreamt of music. He dreamt of Ada McGrath and the strange melodies with which she filled his house. He had built the hut years before when he first bought the land on which it sat. It had only taken a few weeks to construct, using wood from the trees he cut down to clear space. The hut was very basic, one room with a sleeping alcove separated by a curtain, and windows shuttered but glassless. He had intended to build something more substantial some future time, but that time had never arrived. He found it comfortable, nothing wanting in its simplicity.

And now his hut housed a piece of furniture, a musical instrument, more grand than any he had seen in years. When he opened his eyes in the morning the piano was first in his line of vision. He pulled back the lace curtain that hung around his bed, and there it was, waiting to be played, a glorious intrusion in his rough life, like Ada McGrath herself.

George Baines got out of bed, stretching, his body rested. Shafts of early morning sunlight streamed in through the window, dust motes sparkled in the air. Light fell across the rosewood piano and he was drawn toward it. Dust had fallen onto the wood and, lifting his nightshirt over his head, he began to wipe the piano. The smooth wood shone where Baines passed his nightshirt over it. The sun felt warm on his back as he moved around the piano, and he became aware of his nakedness. His movements grew slower and slower until he was no longer just dusting but had begun caressing the piano. It was as though he had become possessed by the piano himself, possessed with gentle desire for the thing and, through it, the woman who played.

GEORGE Baines had lived in New Zealand for more than nine years now. His was an existence that other European settlers thought of as solitary and strange, in his hut, without company. But the other *pakeha* did not include Maoris in their estimations of "people", and Baines' company was kept among the Maori. They knew much more about this wet and bountiful land than any of the settlers. There was much to learn from them, and, like Baines himself, when the living grew scarce, they could take to the sea. He would sometimes make the journey to Nelson and take work on the boats that were heading off to fish. And when he tired of that he would return to his hut and his slow progress with the land.

Baines appreciated the Maoris' way with work, leisure, and the land, their easy peace with themselves and their good-humored tolerance of his ways. At first, Baines had been fascinated by the tattoos—*moko*—that many of the people wore. *Moko* was a highly skilled operation carried out by *tohunga ta moko*—master tattooists—who traveled the country to carry out commissions, like the great wood-carvers whose handmade carving tools were remarkably similar to the *tohunga*'s ornate chisels. One summer the *tohunga* had arrived and, at the urging of Hone and Mana, Baines agreed to have *moko* himself. Partial markings were made on his face. The full tattooing, like the symmetrical patterns adorning Chief Nihe's face, took years of visits, and caused great swelling and pain with the fine chiseling and dyeing of the skin. Baines was unafraid of pain but too restless to sit for the *tohunga* for the hours necessary to complete *moko*. He had grown accustomed to the markings as they were, despite the disdain of the other European settlers slowly increasing in number in the region.

Baines was not Maori, but not true *pakeha* either; yet for a long time he had been content: a part of each world was enough for him. The arrival of Ada McGrath and her piano had disrupted his ease. Baines found himself concerned with what Ada thought of him; he wished that she came to him for more than an opportunity to play her piano. But the lessons would continue. He was glad of that.

*A*UNT MORAG and Nessie approached the woodchop where Stewart worked along the planks across the mud bath that passed for a garden in front of the house. Morag in black, Nessie in brown, Mary in red, all wearing aprons and bonnets and cloaks, they made a sprightly trio against the blackened tree stumps. "Be very careful," Morag warned of the planks. ". . . Careful," echoed Nessie, as though Mary might not have understood.

Ada could hear their voices as she made her separate way along the planks, departing for Baines' lesson as the others arrived.

"I hardly need to give one to you, but there you are anyway," Aunt Morag said to Stewart. Nessie took the basket of invitations from Mary; finding Stewart's invitation, she passed it to Aunt Morag, who then handed it to Stewart officiously. "Don't be late," Morag instructed. "You will see there are two times," she pointed to the invitation, "and since you are accompanying a performer you will need to make the earlier time."

As Morag spoke, Alisdair Stewart began to look away. He had noticed Ada and Flora stepping cautiously along the path, Flora lifting her mother's skirt out of the mud. "Wait," he called. They stopped, turning toward him. "How are the lessons going?"

Ada offered a cautious nod. The lessons were going well; Baines gave her freedom to play as she wished. It gave Ada a small pleasure to think that Alisdair Stewart knew nothing of the bargain that she had made with George Baines. "Getting on all right is he?" Stewart asked. Ada smiled slightly and nodded again, then continued on her way.

"She seems quietened down," commented Aunt Morag, leaning toward her nephew conspiratorially. "Is she more affectionate?" Stewart looked away, embarrassed. "Ah well," said Morag, "slowly, slowly."

ALONG the footpath to George Baines' hut, Flora was unusually quiet. There was a profusion of birds in the air that morning, their song was fervent and loud, and Flora harkened to it. At first she thought that the more curious sounds emanated from some strange bush creature. But she traced the noises to a bird, outrageously plumed, unlike any she had seen. Flora paused to point out the bird to her mother, giving it an imaginary name she thought as vibrant as its feathers, but Ada walked this path as though deaf as well as dumb.

As they neared George Baines' hut the mud began to harden, making it easier to walk. Ada had become accustomed to her skirts always being rimmed with mud. Today it was not raining, and Flynn the dog came out of hiding to greet them, so Flora was off at her games even before Ada knocked on the door. Baines was slow to answer, and when he opened the door he looked at Ada with such intensity that she wondered if he had been drinking. His life in this hut was so irregular that nothing would have surprised her.

By now Ada had accepted the bargain she had made with Baines as another part of her strange new existence. She did not know what he planned, if he planned, for her to earn her keys. Ada was determined to possess her piano again; the nature of the bargain did not concern her: She had always taken pleasure in secrets.

Ignoring Baines, who stood in the door of his hut like a man bewitched, Ada went straight to the piano, spread her music upon it, and sat down to play. George Baines positioned himself near the window; she could see him out of the corner of her eye. Usually he took his place behind her, and she could forget his presence and lose herself completely. But today, as though in anticipation of something, he sat to one side, leaning heavily on his elbow, staring at her, his eyes moving slowly from her hands on the keyboard up her arms, along her neck, to her face.

After she had played for a while, Baines spoke for the first time that day. "Lift your skirt," he said. He spoke slowly, his voice thick.

Ada stopped playing, her small hands resting on the keys. She was not frightened, but shocked. She did not betray her shock to George Baines. Without looking at him, she paused a moment, thinking. So this was his bargain. Then, her face set, expressionless, she lifted her skirt a fraction to show her muddy leather boots and commenced playing again.

George Baines moved uneasily in his chair. He felt as though he were still dreaming and that Ada McGrath had come to him in his sleep. He wanted something from her, he knew not what, and he did not want to force her away. He knew he must be careful not to press her too hard.

"Lift it higher."

Ada scarcely stopped playing this time, lifting her skirt up another inch or two in a quick movement, her hands immediately returning to the keys. George Baines left his seat by the window. Suddenly he was on his hands and knees and then, before she could play another note, he was lying on his side under the piano. Neither knew what would come next. Both felt as though the air had grown heavy and difficult to breathe.

"Higher," Baines said, but Ada pretended not to hear him. He banged his hand twice against the bottom of the piano, and, at this crude and insistent interruption, she stopped playing. "Lift it higher," he said softly.

Ada, taking a deep breath, lifted her skirt and petticoat with its white lace hem above her knees. "Everything," continued Baines, and she brought up the hoops as well, exposing her pantaloons and, beneath them, her black woollen stockings. She glanced under the piano with ill-disguised contempt. She had never seen a man lie on the floor for pleasure before. She had never been asked to do such things. She continued to play, there was nothing else she could do.

George Baines lay back on the hard wooden floor as though comfortable, as though he reclined on large, soft cushions. He was enthralled by Ada's legs, by the deft movements as her feet worked the pedals. Her calves were shapely in their stockings, tucked into small boots with neatly squared toes. He noticed a small hole in the black stocking on Ada's left leg, just beneath the lace. White skin peeped through, Ada's skin, exposed to the

air and Baines' gaze, a chink in the casing of her imperturbable self. Without thinking, he lifted his hand. With
one finger, his nail grubby and toughened, his skin
marked with tobacco and work, he felt her skin through
the hole, cool, soft, smooth—Ada.

Ada started slightly when she felt his touch. She
forced herself to continue to play. By playing she felt she
was giving less of herself to Baines, that he could take less
away. His touch was strange, a slow, gentle caress that
brought her to feel humiliated and oddly constricted in
her throat. She had been touched but once by a man, long
since, and never had she been the object of such profound, direct scrutiny. She felt her face grow hot, and the
place where Baines' slow finger touched her skin tingled.
Ada McGrath kept playing; the ivory piano keys remained cool, their tone precise, unwavering.

*H*ow Ada had loved to listen to Delwar Haussler play.
In those weeks before she herself had played for him,
those weeks when Delwar first came to stay at her father's
house, he had played, and allowed her the luxury of sitting and listening. She watched his long, supple fingers
on the piano keys, his brow furrowing in concentration
during the difficult passages, his frock coat straining
across his back, till Ada feared it would split. Ada knew
well the pleasure of listening.

When Delwar Haussler arrived she had been surprised
to find a young man; she was expecting someone of

McGregor the piano tuner's age, someone ancient and rickety who smelt of pipe smoke and snuff. But Delwar was young in his velvet cap and purple sash. He smiled lightly and frequently and his glamorous conversation was of books, plays, and great composers who lived in fabulous European cities. He had traveled to Vienna to hear the opera, and once she had heard this story Ada made him retell it again and again. The opera house, the singers, the orchestra, the sets, the curtain calls, the very seat in which he sat—she wanted every detail to savor, so far did this world seem from the comfortable confines of her father's house.

Ada was sixteen when Delwar Haussler came, sixteen but nearly seventeen. She had not had much congress with people her own age. There were other young people from the town, children of her father's friends and acquaintances, whom she met at church and on social occasions. She had even been invited to one or two parties, although she had not gone, preferring to allow her muteness to keep her separate. She felt uncomfortable among crowds, and so often people seemed to think it best to shout at Ada as though she were deaf as well as dumb.

But Delwar Haussler soon had made friends in the town, other musicians, young people for the most part. After he had been installed at the McGraths' for several months he began to go out in the evenings occasionally, and soon he had developed his own coterie. Wyston McGrath was not concerned with the nocturnal activities of his daughter's tutor; once a week he would ask Ada how her lessons were progressing, and he never received a report from her that was not to his satisfaction. Given the opportunity, he liked to talk at length with Delwar about Ada's talent. At first Delwar felt it politic to be overly enthusiastic, to inflate a proud father's vanity, but as Ada began to play for him, and as she began to learn to read music and to expand her repertoire, his enthusiasm became genuine.

Delwar's friends in the town were envious of his station, a position in a great house with only one pupil. Delwar did not disabuse them of their illusions, choosing not to mention the fact that each month the household seemed to come nearer to disarray. He had no idea of the state of Wyston McGrath's finances, or of what McGrath might have planned for the future; as long as his wage continued to be deposited at the bank, he was satisfied.

Ada worked hard under the tutelege of Delwar Haussler; he began to instruct her in music theory, harmony, and counterpoint as well. Her father gave them money to order music and books from London and Edinburgh, and Ada continued to extend her knowledge, and with it her delight.

After a year in the McGrath household, Delwar had become a fixture both there and within the musical circles of Aberdeen. He had begun attending church with the McGraths despite his Lutheran upbringing, for the music, and to see his friends in the choir. He became involved in the program of the concert hall, both in the conducting and the playing. He and his friends organized piano recitals and chamber music, and members of the community had begun to request their presence at parties and on special occasions. Soon he had played in all the big houses, and his group had become so popular that they were able to command small fees for their appearances. If appropriate, Ada McGrath would attend these events, sitting near the back of the room and leaving on the arm of her father, or a friend of her father's, immediately after the music finished, these forays into brightly lit salons being both an ordeal and an unusual pleasure for the serious young woman.

Ada felt glad at Delwar's success. He never allowed these other engagements to interfere with their lessons; when she played for him he was always attentive, his mind never strayed. Delwar understood that his success in Aberdeen owed a great deal to the patronage of the McGraths, to whom he was indebted. And Ada was a charming pupil.

One evening, with the permission of her father, Ada accompanied Delwar to a string quartet performance organized by his friends. Delwar had often spoken to Ada of the young violinist, Miss Judith McDougall, who was to perform that evening. He was greatly impressed with her playing and Ada was looking forward to hearing it for herself. They sat together near the front of the room. There was a light buzz in the air; the town had come to expect much of these musical occasions and many people had come to listen.

The quartet arrived, three men dressed in black frock coats and Miss McDougall herself, who wore a black dress with a tight-fitting jacket, cut in a rather daring manner to allow her arms freedom to play, her blond hair swept back off her face. A ripple of excitement passed over the gathering; Aberdeen was unused to female musicians making concert appearances. The crowd felt satisfied by the veneer of sophistication this event bestowed upon them.

As the musicians began to play, Ada noticed Delwar lean forward in his seat, his hands grasping the edges of his chair. She could see he was focusing intently on Miss Judith McDougall. After the music was finished and greeted with enthusiastic applause from the audience, Delwar hurried over to the musicians, leaving Ada on her own in the crowd. As the hall slowly emptied, she remained seated. She could see that not only was Delwar much taken with Miss McDougall's playing, he was also evidently much taken with Miss McDougall herself. Ada stood and walked to the back of the hall where Mr. Beadsley, her father's lawyer, greeted her, asking if he could accompany her home. "Leave the musicians to it, shall we?" he said lightly. Ada walked out to the street rapidly brushing past his proffered arm.

Ada was now eighteen, and there had been no talk of finding her a husband. Her father would always think of Ada as a child. The question occurred from time to time when Beadsley examined Ada's dowry and trust fund, but even he found himself pushing the thought to the back of his mind. Ada was so tiny, solemn, and silent it was easy to pretend she was still a child. And who would marry a mute? What kind of a husband could be found? It was better not to think on it at all.

Ada, of course, experienced none of these confusions. She knew her age, she was sensible of her eighteen years and, in her father's household, without a mother, she sometimes felt years older. She didn't want to be found a husband, though, reasoning that she did not need to marry; she would simply continue with her piano lessons, she would be happy in her father's house with Delwar and nothing else.

But seeing Delwar stand over Miss Judith McDougall, smiling, conversing, oblivious to other people, roused emotions in her that she could not, as yet, name, and she felt threatened in some oblique and dangerous way. Ada walked home quickly, two paces in front of Mr. Beadsley, who called out for her to slow down from time to time. She ignored him. On arriving at the house, she went straight up to her room, not waiting in the music room for Delwar as she sometimes did, where they might have hot milk or cocoa while Delwar talked about the evening's music.

All next morning Ada hid herself in her room, inventing work where there had been none before. When the time came for her afternoon lesson, she went down to the music room and, before Delwar arrived, began to play loud, discordant music, an improvisation of the kind in which she used to indulge endlessly before she learned to read music. After a few minutes Delwar entered the room. "What are you playing?" he shouted over her noise. She was aware without looking that he was smiling, so she played even more loudly, all the strings within the piano reverberating. Delwar came and stood beside the piano, but she refused to look at him, concentrating on the fierce movement of her fingers on the keys. He was shouting again, but she could not hear his words. She continued to play. When he reached one hand down to begin to strike a few bass notes himself, as though he wanted to join in with her cacophony, Ada stopped playing abruptly and brought the lid of the keyboard smartly down, narrowly missing his fingers. She stood and glared up at him, turning suddenly as if to flee the room. He grabbed her wrist and said, gently, "What are you doing?" He had never seen her temper displayed.

Ada kicked out the piano stool and tried to wrench her arm from his grip, but Delwar hung on. "I do believe," he spoke slowly as the notion dawned on him, "that you are jealous." Ada fought, twisting more furiously. "I do believe that you are jealous of Miss Judith McDougall, Miss Ada McGrath." She gasped and looked up at him, her face flushed. Still clutching her wrist, Delwar Haussler leaned down and kissed Ada's lips. It was a soft kiss, despite the violence of the situation. He loosened his grip, and Ada dropped suddenly onto the bench. Delwar sat beside her. They had never sat side by side on the piano bench before; there was only just room for two. He began to play quietly, a piece she knew well. As he reached for the higher notes, his arm brushed against hers. She did not move back to allow him more room. Ada McGrath stayed right where she was on the bench, with Delwar Haussler, seated and playing the piano, next to her. *"Adagio,"* he said quietly, "slowly. Slowly."

Chapter 7

THERE were two women at the river hole when Baines went down to bathe and wash his clothes. Their children played in a canoe, and a young Maori man named Tahu lolled on a branch above the water. They watched Baines, commenting as he worked, alternating between great seriousness and hilarity. One of the women, Hira, who wore her black hair in a long plait and had *moko* on her bottom lip, crouched on a branch that swung out over the water, intent on giving Baines some motherly advice.

"You need a wife," Hira told Baines. "It's not good having it sulk between your legs for the rest of its life." Baines smiled, and the children giggled as did Waimara in her burlap shirt.

"You no worry, Peini," said Tahu coyly, using the Maori name for Baines. "I save you." Tahu dropped one leg seductively in the water. He wore a necklace of shells, a colored cloth wrapped around his narrow hips.

"I have a wife," Baines replied, their conversation alternating between English and the Maori language.

"It's all right," said Tahu, playing with his hair. "I save her too."

"Quiet!" Hira berated him. "Balls were wasted on you."

"And you would know," replied Tahu saucily. Baines laughed.

Hira leaned forward, "Where's your wife?"

"My wife?" said Baines. "Oh, she has a life of her own. At Hull in England."

"She must be ugly? . . ." asked Hira. Baines did not reply. ". . . for you to run away. You need another wife. Such a treasure," she gestured to his penis, "should not sleep on your stomach at night."

The women dissolved into laughter and Baines, smiling, looked back down at his washing.

$\mathcal{A}$DA had scarcely begun to play that afternoon when Baines, feeling an intolerable urgency, said to her, "Undo your dress." Ada McGrath looked up from the piano with such ferocity that he wondered if he had pushed her too far. "I want to see your arms," he continued, reasonably, as though this was an everyday request.

Ada nodded ruefully, parting her lips as if to say she should have known that this would be next. Baines sat in a dark corner of the hut where Ada could not see his face clearly. With restrained obedience—a bargain was a bargain after all—she lifted her silver case and pencil from her neck.

Ada rose, undoing the buttons of her short jacket. She pulled her arms out of the sleeves and moved away from the piano to hang it up. Underneath she wore a soft, white bodice with short sleeves above her narrow corset. The pellucid flesh of her neck and shoulder now exposed seemed vulnerable and when she turned back to the piano, Baines' gaze fell on her back where the bodice scooped low across her thin white shoulderblades. "Play," he said.

George Baines stood and took off his shirt. Beneath it he wore a gray long-sleeved undershirt. Baines thought Ada's skin so pale it seemed transparent. A delicate network of blue-green veins crisscrossed along the soft underpart of her arm. The backs of her hands, the only part of her body exposed to the sun, were quite brown in comparison. Baines was mesmerized by this contrast.

Ada began to play. She heard George Baines walk up behind her, the floorboards creaking under his weight, and she felt his breath on her neck. He bent low and touched her, running his square, callused fingers along the tender length of her underarm. She stopped playing, raising her hands to the bare skin of her throat. "Two keys," he said, speaking into her ear, escalating the terms of their bargain.

Ada played the first few notes of a hesitant melody. George Baines rested his hand under Ada's wrist—so narrow, the bones so fine. She played and again his hand lingered along the skin of her arm and up into the warm hollow beneath her shoulder. Then he stepped back and

Ada, listening closely, heard him discard his undershirt, dropping it on the floor. Ada stared straight ahead, not wanting to hear, see, or feel, as Baines came near and began to run his hands gently, slowly, along her neck and her shoulders, which were uncovered, bared, to him. She forced herself to play but then, as he touched her, she felt she could stand no more. Unnerved by his intensity, she began to play a contrite and mocking jig, brisk, almost comical. Baines felt suddenly ridiculous. The mood was broken, she had broken it. He took his hand away from her skin and retreated into the darkness at the far end of the room, his hands on his hips. Ada continued to play, victorious. She had won herself a respite.

FLORA stood patiently on a chair while Aunt Morag and Nessie worked at fitting her bodice with the wire angel wings she was to wear for the Nativity play. The two women were attempting to learn some of the hand gestures with which Flora and her mother communicated.

Flora spoke and signed simultaneously. "I shall listen hard at rehearsal, because I live too far away to go often." Nessie tried to mimic Flora's quick hand movements.

"Which sign is the word 'rehearsal'?" asked Aunt Morag. Flora demonstrated again and they tried to copy her, momentarily confused when Flora stopped to scratch her arm. "Oh," said Morag, giving up, "I can't imagine a fate worse than being dumb."

"To be deaf?" offered Nessie, grimacing dramatically.

"Oh aye, deaf too—terrible." Morag shuddered. "Awful."

"Actually," said Flora, while Nessie and Aunt Morag went back to work on her wings, "to tell you the whole truth, Mumma says most people speak rubbish and it's not worth the listen."

Morag and Nessie exchanged looks. "Well," said Morag stiffly, "that is a strong opinion."

"Aye," replied Flora. "It's unholy."

Morag and Nessie paused; it frightened them to hear such weird, bold words spoken by a child, and in so proud a tone.

*A*LISDAIR STEWART's expression was tense, his bearing rigid, as he and Baines confronted Chief Nihe, the Maori leader, and his people. Stewart wished to purchase some of their land and had brought Baines along to negotiate. Baines could not fathom Stewart's obsession with the acquisition of land, but he was prepared to act as mediator for the *pakeha* and the Maori. Stewart knew he would never have Baines' facility with these people and their impossible language; he did not want it, although it pained him to use a go-between and have other men know his business.

The Maori chief was dressed in an European tweed suit and bowler hat, with symmetrical *moko* patterns emanating from his mouth and eyes. "The rivers and the burial caves of our ancestors lie within these lands," the chief said in Maori, with a slow and powerful deliberateness, his arm gesturing broadly to indicate all directions. "Tell that to him, Peini." Chief Nihe pointed at Stewart.

While the chief spoke, Stewart muttered to Baines, "What are they saying? Are they selling?"

The old man continued: "Are you saying we should sell the bones of our ancestors?"

"Offer the blankets for half the land," whispered Stewart. Baines nodded.

"Never, there is no price you can pay," said the chief before Baines had a chance to translate.

"Twelve," said Stewart to the Maori man, smiling nervously, holding up his fingers to indicate the number.

"*Te, kaumarua paraikete mo te tahi hawhe o te whenua nei*— He'll give you twelve blankets for half the land," explained Baines. Hone, the chief's son, stepped forward and spat on the ground that lay between them.

"Offer the guns, Baines, offer the guns," Stewart urged, his nervousness increasing. Baines translated as Stewart pulled off the blanket that had been covering the guns and stood one on its butt, smiling uneasily as he showed it off.

Chief Nihe uttered a short vehement speech, which Baines did not translate, before he and his people rose as one and left the two *pakeha.*

𝓛ADEN with the spurned blankets and guns, Stewart and Baines made their way back from the unsuccessful negotiations along the edge of the property for which Stewart had traded the piano. "What do they want it for?" he complained of the Maoris. "They don't cultivate it, burn it back, anything. How do they even know it's theirs?"

Baines slowed to a halt beside a freshly placed fence post. Stewart fell silent and watched Baines a little anxiously. Baines walked on to the next post, touching the newly split wood, thinking of the land he had given up. "I thought I might as well mark it out," Stewart explained tentatively.

"Yes," said Baines, "why not?"

They continued to climb. "Ada says you're doing well with the piano. I'll come and hear you play. What do you play?"

"Nothing just yet."

"No?" Stewart replied, puzzled, fearing that Ada was failing in her side of the bargain. He did not feel he could trust her, although he had need to. They carried on climbing, the rest of their expedition made in mutual brooding.

A D A took off her short jacket, so she could play in her bodice as had been arranged. It seemed natural that as each step was taken there would be no going back to the way things had been before. She placed the jacket over the back of a chair. In truth, not wearing it let her move more freely as she played, but Ada would never admit that to George Baines.

Baines had greeted her without speaking. Ada thought he spoke very little for a person who could speak at all, but she had grown accustomed to his silences and, despite the compromises she was being forced to make each visit, she still looked forward to the time when she would own her piano. For Ada that was still the most important thing, the only thing.

While she played, lowering her body nearer to the keys, shutting out the rest of the world, Baines stood and walked to the chair where Ada's jacket hung. He picked up the garment, smoothing the cloth, and carried it back to where he sat, directly behind Ada. Baines held the jacket close, it was still warm from her body. Eyes closed, he lifted it toward his face, and sniffed the cloth. He lowered it, and opened it out, splaying the sleeves that seemed so narrow, so small in his hands. Ada wore this material next to her skin. He fingered the stitching, touched the buttons, his eyes still closed. He lifted it and buried his face in it yet again. Like the piano, the cloth was permeated with her scent.

Ada turned slightly as she played, aware of George Baines' movements. When she saw what he was doing she stopped short, appalled by his odd, sensual pleasure-taking. To bury his face in her jacket as if it were alive: This was a strange thing for a man to do. It was too much. Ada swung around on her seat and held out her hand for the jacket, her expression stern and censorious. Baines ignored her, his eyes closed, his expression lost, not noticing the music had ceased. Ada walked over to him, snatching the jacket from his hands. He looked up, startled, and she hesitated, waiting a moment to see what next he would do, before turning away.

Baines rose and followed Ada. Abruptly, he grabbed her by the arm, twisting her body toward him. Taking hold of the sleeves of her white bodice and jerking downward, he tore the material, exposing her pale shoulders and breast. He pressed his face into the hollow at the base of her neck, kissing her desperately. Ada gasped, a soft sound, not loud enough to alert Flora. Baines began hauling Ada across the floor; it became terribly clear that he was taking her to his bed. She struggled against him, pulling in the opposite direction. This was much, much more than she was expecting. As he sat on the bed, Baines released her, and Ada pulled her bodice together to cover her shoulders again, turning away toward the uncertain sanctuary of the piano, clutching her jacket.

"Ada," Baines said, his voice low, full of strained exasperation, but calm. "Four keys."

Ada held up her hand, fingers and thumb outstretched, and mouthed "Five," continuing to straighten her bodice.

"Why five?" asked Baines. "I just want to lie."

Ada looked at Baines, her heart pounding, her eyes steadfast. She would not lower her terms.

"All right, all right, five," said George Baines, holding up his hands in resignation. He lay down on the bed, smiling, his big face open and playful, and patted the space next to him as though it were the most natural thing in the world.

Ada McGrath looked at George Baines. She could not believe her bargain had taken her to this. Drawing a deep breath, she pulled her bodice together again and laid down on her stomach on the bed, next to Baines.

After a hushed moment Baines began to caress Ada's shoulders, pushing down the sleeves of her torn bodice once more. She closed her eyes, not breathing, then opened them when she felt his lips brush against her skin. He kissed her back, her ear, gently pushing his face down onto her neck, his movements soft with feeling. Ada lay perfectly still, high color in her cheeks. Then, suddenly aware of her stillness, George Baines too became still. They paused, hearing the bird song that came from outside, the sound of their own breath. Ada felt alarmed by the strange, dizzy sensations that rose through her body. It scared and shamed her to be feeling anything at all.

Baines raised himself up over her shoulders, wondering if Ada's face might betray her feelings. She seized that moment to rise from the bed, dragging her hand away from his as she traversed the room. From the bed, Baines watched as Ada ran the back of her hand noiselessly over the polished ivory keys of the piano, a gesture showing affection never afforded to him. Baines went toward Ada. He slammed down the piano lid in a gesture full of ownership, forcing Ada to remove her hand from where it lingered over the keys. Ada picked up her jacket and put

it on once again, close to tears over his cruel unpredict-
able action and her own perilous situation.

Throughout the long walk to Stewart's house, Ada's
thoughts raged. What was happening to her? In all her
years of silence she had never wished that she could speak
but now she wished she could read what lay behind
George Baines' own silence. His attention flattered her
pride, she knew this and felt it dangerous. But having
proceeded thus far with the arrangement, she knew herself determined to carry it through, come what may, and
win back her piano. No cost to her would be as dear as
the loss of her piano.

Preoccupied as she was, Ada ignored Flora, whose
chatter was all of the Christmas play, which was to be
presented in a few days' time. Flora knew her mother did
not listen but she talked on regardless. She did not like
the way her mother seemed altered of late. "And I'm to
play the Baby Jesus next year Mumma, and everyone will
have to do as I say," she essayed, but Ada did not hear.

In his hut George Baines lingered in a state of bitter-
sweet torment for as long as he thought he could still
detect Ada's scent. He imagined her making her way
home through the bush, away from him. A black and desolate void threatened to engulf him. Why did she not remain with him, lying warm against his body?

$\mathcal{T}$HE day of the play finally arrived, and Flora could
scarcely contain her excitement. Ada helped her assemble

the costume that Aunt Morag had finished only that morning. As Ada untied the long strips of rag, releasing the ringlets that Flora had always coveted, the child sang her favorite carol, "The Holly and Ivy." It seemed strange to have Christmas at a time of year when the weather was so warm, but Flora had quickly become unastonished by the stark contrasts and uncertainties of their new life. She loved her angel wings and looked forward to making her stage debut.

It was a golden evening as Stewart, in his best shirt, jacket, and trousers, prepared the horse and cart to take his small family to the mission school hall. On arrival, people were being ferried through the deep mud in wheelbarrows, children in their costumes lifted and passed from hand to hand, like buckets of water to a fire, while the church bell rang.

Inside was chaos. Extra chairs were being brought in to accommodate the crowd. Backstage, the Sunday school teacher gathered the children together, reminding them of the order of the songs, checking their hair and lip color, making sure they had all made use of the privy. Some of the children peered out through the strategically cut holes in the curtain at the gathering crowd. Two of the women helpers were putting a little coloring on each of the angels' bright faces, while two angels were being smacked for dipping their white-gloved hands in the bucket of stage blood so carefully concocted by Reverend Campbell. All around milled members of the dramatic society who were taking part in the Reverend's play.

A crowd of about forty people had gathered in the mission hall, including Chief Nihe and ten or more of his people in their best European dress. Everyone was chatting gaily, except the Maoris, who waited solemnly for events to begin, not knowing what to expect. Aunt Morag organized the placement of the new seats. At the door of the hall, some men stood greeting people as they entered. George Baines arrived, looking odd in a top hat he had excavated from amongst his possessions. An appearance by Baines at such an occasion was utterly novel, and he himself felt painfully awkward.

"Look who's here," said one of the men, "the musical Mr. Baines."

"What are you going to play for us tonight, George . . . 'Twinkle, twinkle'?" asked another man.

"How about a little tinkle, tinkle, eh George?"

Baines blinked and removed his hat. He ignored the men, passing by without greeting. The teasing continued as he surveyed the room, searching for Ada. Still he ignored their comments, uneasy. Stewart's aunt bustled over, festive red ribbons adorning her elaborately styled hair. Taking his arm, she escorted Baines away from the door.

"Perhaps you would like to turn the pages for Nessie?" Morag suggested. "She's playing for the children." She led Baines over to the piano.

"I'm in costume," explained Nessie, lowering her eyes. She was wearing a white dress with a wedding veil.

"I'm very impressed that you've taken up the piano,"

said Morag to Baines, as though it were her concern. She turned the pages of the music book. "Now where's this song?"

Just then Baines noticed Ada McGrath entering the hall, accompanied by Alisdair Stewart. She looked glorious in red silk, the skin of her breast and throat lucent; he was taken aback by her uncommon beauty. She made her way along a row of chairs toward a seat, halting suddenly as she felt the intensity of Baines' gaze upon her. It was shocking for Ada to see Baines in company, and she found herself angry that he should have come at all. In the dark, wooded privacy of his hut, their meetings had a distant quality, as if everything that happened there belonged to another world. Seeing him here tonight broke that spell. Baines was real, as was his strange obsession, as were her own intimate compromises, all discomfortingly real.

Without speaking, Baines walked away from Morag and Nessie, who looked after him, amazed by his lack of manners. He made his way along the row behind Ada and Stewart and then sat in the seat next but one to Ada, behind red-haired twins resplendent in their Christmas-play costumes. Ada ignored Baines as thoroughly as he had ignored the men at the door.

"George, excuse me," said one of those same men. "How about 'Mary had a little lamb.' Baa-baa."

"Or a polka. Come on, George, what's it to be, hmm?" added another.

Stewart turned to look at the men teasing Baines.

"Fools," he muttered under his breath. "Come on George, move along." Baines began to move into the seat next to Ada when, turning quickly, she placed her hand forcefully on the seat, silencing him with an accusing stare. George Baines, rebuffed, sat back, pained by so direct and confident a snub.

"Ladies and gentleman," announced the Reverend from the stage, "take your seats. We're about to begin." The curtains opened then, and all the children filed nervously on to the stage, costumed as clouds and angels, clutching their candles and their staffs of stars and moons. The audience gave a collective sigh at their lovely innocence. The children stood in a group singing with great solemnity, but, struck with shyness, their voices were so small as barely to be heard. As Flora came forward to the front of the stage, Alisdair Stewart took Ada's hand in his, and she did not resist. Stewart smiled with pleasure. Ada looked down at their hands joined together and smiled as well. Glancing to the side, she could see George Baines had witnessed this display of affection. She felt a small flame of satisfaction as she imagined his hurt. Her husband squeezed her hand. George Baines, glowering, suddenly quite out of control, stood and left. Replete with stubborn victory, Ada watched him go.

Next, the Reverend came on wearing harlequin tights and a large, frilly neckpiece, carrying a tray of burning candles that lit his theatrically painted face dramatically. The tale enacted was "Bluebeard," a parable the European audience found fearsome though familiar. "And so the young maid came upon each and all of Bluebeard's missing wives, their severed heads still bleeding, their eyes still crying."

As he narrated, Nessie, acting the young bride, appeared. Through the sheet that served as a backdrop hung the heads of Bluebeard's previous wives. The piano accompaniment jangled with suspense while the audience shrieked appreciatively. Nessie crept along the stage illuminating each of the severed heads with her tray of candles. Backstage, Aunt Morag was busy with the ladle, providing the blood that dripped down the wives' necks and onto the backcloth. Moving between the corpses, Morag peered out at Nessie through a peephole in the curtain. "Slow down, Nessie," she hissed, "slow down."

"But hush!" intoned the Reverend. "Who comes?"

Standing, Nessie gasped and blew out her candles with a flourish. The extravagant noise of a door creaking open was followed by heavy footsteps, which resounded around the hall. Nessie froze, her eyes rolling wildly. The huge, bearded shadow of Bluebeard moved into view behind the backdrop.

"I'm home early, my sweet wife," called out the enormous silhouetted figure, its great stomach and long arms effectively menacing. A violin screeched ominously. "Where art thou?"

Nessie, clutching a huge key, moved forward until she too stood in silhouette behind the backdrop. "Ooh, husband, what a surprise!" she trilled.

"Yes wife, a surprise indeed," said Bluebeard, taking

the key from her hand. "So now you know my secret!" His long, pointed fingers threatened her. The children were all now seated in the audience, still in costume, and, wide-eyed, they gasped in unison. Ada hugged Flora closer to her side.

"No, no," squealed Nessie.

"You, the youngest . . . and sweetest . . . of all my wives . . . must be prepared . . ." his voice rose, along with his axe, which he held suspended in the air above Nessie who cowered, her arms raised in supplication, "to DIE!"

In the audience there was a murmur of real apprehension. Two of the young Maori warriors from Chief Nihe's clan, Hone and Mana, half rose from their seats.

"*Aue! Ha aha ra tenei?*—Hey! What is this?" whispered Hone. "Is this murder?"

"No, no, wait please," Nessie pleaded on the stage. A cluster of Maori men rose to their feet as one.

"I shall not wait!" proclaimed Bluebeard.

"No," screamed Nessie.

"Bare your neck," growled Bluebeard. As the evil figure raised his axe again, the Maoris moved forward. "*Pokoko-hua*—coward!" shouted Mana, "bite on my club!" And with that he ran through the audience. All of Bluebeard's dead wives opened their eyes and began to scream. "Let's see how this feels up your arse!" he shouted, waving his club and climbing onto the stage, followed by other Maori men.

The audience parted swiftly and ran to the side of the hall, while on the stage there was much confusion and screaming that was genuine now. The warriors had Blue-beard cornered and whimpering, an umbrella held spear-like over him. Chief Nihe and some of the other Maoris, his daughters included, remained seated. Nihe stamped his stick on the floor, his great voice booming out, *"Hoki mai!*—Enough! Enough! Come back here."

Later, Chief Nihe and his party, offended warriors included, were taken backstage, where the theatrical devices were demonstrated—the blood bucket, the paper axe, the splits in the sheets. One by one Aunt Morag introduced Bluebeard's dead wives to the Maori men, "This is Mrs. Williams, this is Mrs. Parsons, this is Mrs. Reid, this is Miss . . ." she paused when she reached the unmarried ladies, ". . . Miss Palmer, this is Miss Kerr." The Maoris bowed and shook the women's hands graciously. "That is very, very nice," Aunt Morag concluded, to no one in particular.

Chapter 8

GEORGE BAINES had spent long, stifling hours brooding over Ada McGrath after his precipitate departure from the mission hall. Now he sat silent, his mood heavy in the room. Ada played the thirteenth key once and turned to him for instructions. Baines was slumped in a pose of dejection, his head supported by his fist. He seemed quite altered, sulky and distant. When he looked up Ada nodded and gestured expectantly. "Do what you like," he said, his voice loose with fatigue. "Play what you like." He sighed, feeling that he could not have—and should not want—entry to the silent world of this married, self-contained woman.

Ada was perplexed by this odd change in Baines. She wondered if his having seen Alisdair Stewart hold her hand was responsible; it was startling to find her caprice should have such an effect. A little uncertainly, she set about her playing, going back to the same melody she had been developing and embellishing for some weeks now, a rising and falling rhythm expressing some of the tumult and confusion in her heart and mind. She played quite quickly today in rapid four/four time, bending toward the keyboard. After a little she turned; something was wrong. Her hands lingered, playing a few random notes as she realized Baines was not there. Surprised, she rose from her seat, full of sudden anxiety, fearing that Baines might renege on their agreement when there were now less than half the keys remaining. She walked quietly, the creaking of the floorboards loud in the sudden silence, trying to discern where Baines might be, listening for his breath. Moving slowly, her skirts whispering, she reached the red lace curtain that sheltered his bed, paused, then peered behind. Nothing. She continued along the room to the second curtain. Hesitating, she drew it to one side and at once stepped back, gasping at what she had seen.

Behind her George Baines pulled the curtain aside. He was there, naked. Ada had never seen a man without clothes before. George Baines stood in a narrow shaft of sunlight. His body was squat, broad, and vigorous, his thick-ribbed musculature clearly defined by the light. He stared at Ada, unblinking, and said, "I want to lie together without clothes on." Ada did not know where to look. She clutched her hand to her mouth. "How many would that be?" he asked, his voice steady, convincing.

Ada looked at the floor, then straight at George Baines. She was torn between wanting to spurn Baines and his insolent presumption and wanting to exploit this opportunity to earn precious keys. Without further deliberation, she held up all the fingers of one hand twice.

"Yes," said George Baines firmly, "ten keys."

Ada held up both her hands showing ten fingers again, as though in final confirmation of the price. And then she inhaled sharply, shocked by her own consent.

George Baines drew the curtain back from his bed. He sat down, resting one arm across his knee, and looked on as Ada began to undress.

In the forest, Flora was lost in her imagination, riding the branch of a tree as though it were a horse. She had rigged a bridle and reins and sat sidesaddle, humming the song she had learned for the play as she rode her pony Gabriel across the hills. With Gabriel, Flora did not feel so alone.

Ada lifted her dress over her head, revealing her bodice and corset, pantaloons and stockings, and the awkward crinoline cage. She moved her hands to the hoops, to the fasteners on her stays.

Suddenly aware that the piano music had stopped, Flora slid down from her saddle and climbed up the bank toward the hut.

Inside, Ada was naked too now, all the artillery of her clothing shed. After smoothing the covers on George Baines' bed and spreading her petticoat upon it, she climbed over and settled herself upright against a red cushion, knees raised protectively. In her skin she seemed even smaller, vulnerable without the impenetrable carapace of her stiff layers of clothing. Very gently, Baines drew her legs forward, guiding her shoulders, bringing her body close to his on the bed.

Flora climbed the veranda steps to investigate the mysterious silence. She stopped humming and peered through various cracks and holes in the irregularly built hut. Her vision was restricted, but she could see parts of bodies, pale skin glowing in the darkness. Mr. Baines seemed to be lying on top of her mother. Challenged and inquisitive, she continued to spy through yet another hole in the wall. She heard George Baines murmuring softly, telling secrets to her mother, secrets that Flora knew that she herself would not be allowed to share.

Ada could not move, and Baines did nothing to make her wish to do so, his touch good and gentle, his kisses tender. She felt paralyzed and yet at repose; his skin was warm, pliant and alive, nothing like the piano keys beneath her fingertips. She let her hand lie where he had placed it, quietly impassive. After a while, Baines rolled away. They stared at each other as though trying to fathom what the other might feel. Then Ada rose to dress.

THE next day, Flora and three small Maori children whom she had befriended played among a sunny grove of pine trees. Three Maori women were smoking and chatting in the shade, one holding in her lap a pig that was kept as a favored pet. The children were playing a game that consisted of rubbing themselves up and down against tree trunks, kissing and hugging the bark. When one child shouted "Next!" they all swapped trees. The game had an edge of promiscuity to it as they continued to move from tree to tree, two or more of them sometimes kissing the same tree.

Not noticed by the happy party, Stewart walked through the woods toward Flora. When he realized the nature of their game, he grabbed his stepdaughter and pulled her away from the tree upon which she had just planted a great kiss.

"Never behave like that, never, nowhere," he said to Flora harshly, struggling to contain his temper while the Maori women mocked his distress. "You are greatly shamed. You have shamed those trunks." Clicking their tongues and shaking their heads, the women watched him drag the child away. Flora's cheeks burned with humiliation. There seemed nothing she could do to please her mother or this man.

Stewart brought Flora back to the pine trees some hours later and instructed her to wash with soapy water each and every tree that she had shamed. At first she was a little tearful, but as she scrubbed vigorously she became quite cross. When Stewart reappeared she said, proud with knowledge she knew had certain value, "I know why Mr. Baines can't play the piano."

"You've missed some here," said Alisdair Stewart, pointing at the tree.

"She never gives him a turn. She just plays what she

pleases. Sometimes she doesn't play at all." Flora's pinafore was wet with suds.

Stewart looked at Flora evenly. "When's the next lesson?"

"Tomorrow," Flora replied.

$\mathcal{T}$HE following day was very windy. The noise of the bush was tremendous, the tops of the trees thrashed in fierce gusts of wind, smaller branches crashed to the ground where ferns whirled like dervishes. The two women pressed on through a great barrage of sound, creaking and rushing; Ada's long cape flapping uncontrollably while Flora's little one stood out on end. Birds flew on mad, wind-battered courses, swooped up then strangely drawn down.

Ada and Flora arrived at Baines' hut to find the piano being carried away by a group of Maori men. The men chanted while they heaved the great instrument down the steps of the veranda. One bowler-hatted man did nothing but walk beside it hammering the keys in a kind of rhythmic accompaniment to the chanting, which grew louder with each heave. Panicking at this unexpected turn of events, Ada hurried into the hut with Flora lagging behind.

Inside, Hira was cooking for George Baines. Both she and Baines stopped their activity and looked up as Ada entered. She seemed distraught, signing emphatically to indicate what she had seen, demanding an explanation.

She was much more expressive than usual; the only person who regularly saw her this animated was Flora. Ada stopped signing and paced the floor, trying to compose herself. She was experiencing a bewildering tide of emotion; as she struggled to stay calm she realized with a start that her overwhelming feeling was one of rejection. Her piano was being expelled from the hut of George Baines, herself with it, and this did not make her as happy as she might have thought.

She could still hear the men chanting as they carried her piano away.

"I have given the piano back to you," said George Baines. He was standing now, his expression both concerned and pained. Ada looked at him. What could this mean? "I've had enough," he continued.

Ada opened her mouth and made a strangled sound that conveyed great dismay and confusion. Her breath came quickly. He'd had enough of what—her or the piano? Her playing, her presence: He was breaking off their bargain. She felt dizzy, thrown off balance by this provocative reversal.

Baines came toward her, turning his body and moving Ada to one side in order to prevent Flora and Hira from hearing. She saw how he was disheveled and pale. "This arrangement is making you a whore and me wretched," he whispered. Ada stared at the floor. "I want you to care for me, but you can't."

He returned to where he had been seated by the fire

with Hira. "It's yours. Leave." Ada looked at him, her heart heavy with resentment and fear.

"Go on, go!" George Baines hissed angrily.

Adjusting her bonnet and lifting her skirt, Ada McGrath fled.

The Maoris were making quick progress with the piano, talking animatedly, telling bold jokes to alleviate the strain. Flora and Ada walked in front of them, concentrating on the progress of the instrument. The men had covered the piano with blankets and seemed to be as careful as they were quick. Ada, rushing from one emotion to the next, felt sudden, clear happiness about the piano; it was hers.

From a distance, Alisdair Stewart saw the small parade advancing through the trees. He had been on his way to make an unannounced inspection of the lesson that Ada was to give George Baines today. He was disconcerted to come upon the piano in the woods instead.

"Stop right there!" he barked. Nearly running, he crossed the rough terrain. "This isn't yours . . ." he said to Ada and Flora, speaking as though they were both children. "What are you doing with the piano? Hmm?"

Flora and Ada exchanged looks, Ada uncertain how to respond. Flora spoke for her: "He's given it to us." Her little face was open, puzzled that he did not share their pleasure. In contrast, Ada's countenance was now closed, exhibiting no emotion. She stared at him blankly, impossible to read.

Stewart rushed after the Maoris. "Put it down," he commanded. "Put it down!" He returned, moving near to his wife, and lowering his voice. "Very cunning Ada," he said, pointing at her, "but I've seen through you. I'm not going to lose the land this way." He could not understand why his wife should vex him so. Again he felt almost as though the piano was proving to be a curse on their marriage. "Stay there!" he shouted as he pounded back up the path.

Hira was sitting on the steps of Baines' hut, guarding the door. "George don't want to see nobody," she said. "He's sick." Stewart stopped, leaning on the wooden banister, breathless. Hira motioned him closer. "You got *Tupeka* for Hira?"

Stewart knew she was asking for tobacco. "No," he said abruptly, moving past her, over to Baines' window. He pushed his hand through the glassless opening and brushed the curtain to one side. "Baines," he said.

Baines was lying on his back on his bed, one arm over his eyes.

"Baines, look," said Stewart. "I don't think you should have given up the piano. Now I'll make sure that you're properly taught, you know, with music written on sheets and so on." He was anxious to repair any damage wrought by his wife's erratic behavior.

"I don't want to learn," George Baines said, sitting up listlessly. He did not look well.

"You don't want to learn?" Stewart repeated.

"No."

Stewart paused. "What does this do to our bargain? I can't afford the piano if you mean me to pay."

"No, no payment. I have given it back."

"Well, I'm not sure that I want it myself," Stewart said, plainly.

"It was more to your wife that I gave it," Baines replied, walking toward the hearth.

"Oh," said Stewart, "oh, I see." He felt foolish suddenly, awkward in the face of Baines' magnanimity. "Well, I expect she will appreciate it."

Unable to think of any further conversation—he felt he had been rash to interpret Flora's revelation so hastily—Alisdair Stewart made his way home. His relief that the land deal remained in place was huge. Eighty acres was not enormous, but the stream that ran through it was important: He needed that parcel of land to feed water to his lower pastures. Now that the piano was being returned to Ada, without cost or inconvenience to himself, he felt the venture a complete success. His wife would have her piano, and he had not been weak; he had not given in to her temper. Still, perhaps, her pleasure with the piano would soften her toward him. The memory of holding her hand at the play had been with him at odd times as he sat at rest from work or while readying himself for bed. The tiny darling woman's hand warm and gentle held in his like a little dove, soft and creaturelike. He longed to hold her in his arms, but this seemed yet an unconscionable distance to travel, and he pushed the thought back into obedience. They had held hands, that was good, and at the moment he wished only for a time when he might hold her hand again.

The piano had been delivered safely, but as Stewart had recently been on a supply trip, he had no cash available to pay the Maori men for their labor. All he had was a jar of buttons, a currency that, in the early days of trading, the Maoris had accepted. Now his offering only angered them.

"Stick your buttons up your arse, you bastard," one shouted, although Stewart could not understand his words. "We aren't children."

The others began to shout as well.

"This is all I have," Stewart replied, clearly discomfited. And before he could stop them, one of the young men, Tahu, had snatched his jar of buttons and run off, holding it in the air above his head. "Bring that back!" Stewart shouted, ineffectually. The older Maoris left slowly, muttering angrily.

Oblivious to the commotion outside, Ada lifted the lid of the piano and began to play chords, checking for damage, listening to the tone.

Stewart came in, closing the door behind him. "Is it all right?" he asked. "Why don't you play something?"

Ada stood back from the piano. She was reluctant to play for the man who had bargained her piano away. She gestured to Flora who sat down, pleased at the opportunity to perform for an audience. "What will I play?" she asked, shyly.

Stewart glanced at Ada, who stood blankly by the window. "Play a jig," he suggested.

Flora looked to her mother. "Do I know any jigs?" Ada ignored her daughter, sunk in her own thoughts.

"Play a song, then . . ." said Stewart.

Flora began to sing and play a mournful Scottish tune. After listening to the first phrases, Ada walked past the piano and out through the door of the house. She had to get away from the piano and all that it meant: Baines, his sudden rejection, her impossible marriage. She felt confused, the piano somehow the locus of that confusion. Stewart watched her leave as he thumped his hand on the piano, keeping time as Flora sang. Moving toward the window, he watched as Ada wandered amid the ghostly blackened trunks. Flora broke off playing. Exasperated by this unresponsive, enigmatic woman, Stewart said, "Why won't she play? We get the thing back, she just wanders off." Flora did not reply, it was not as though Stewart spoke to her directly. She too felt baffled and hurt by her mother's remote mien. "Well, keep playing," Stewart said, grimly slapping the top of the piano while Flora continued her dirge.

Ada kept walking, her face dark and puzzled. She stopped and looked toward the house. There was Alisdair Stewart in the window, watching. Without thinking, she looked away and then found herself turning irresistibly toward George Baines' hut. She peered deep into the bush, as though by concentrating hard enough she could see beyond the trees, discover what was troubling her heart so. Turning away again, toward the burnt and smoldering trees on her husband's land, she walked on.

Ada knew that the direction in which her mind traveled was unnavigable. George Baines was not her husband; now he was no longer her pupil either. There was no legitimate reason to visit him. Although she tried not to, Ada found herself always comparing the two men now. At times she felt more like she worked for Alisdair Stewart than was wife to him; they were still formal and stiff with one another, that had not changed. Would she be able to forgive him now that the piano was hers again, now that her carnal bargain with George Baines had been terminated? She turned and walked on, striving to keep herself from the path to Baines' hut. She was restless and greatly disturbed and knew of no way to ease this feeling. Arms folded about herself in a sad embrace, she continued to pace back and forth across the funereal terrain in front of her husband's house.

$\mathcal{A}$DA looked at her piano from where she sat in the kitchen breakfasting. A beam of morning light fell across the instrument, highlighting the polished sheen of the rosewood. She moved toward the piano, running a cloth across the top, then brushed the back of her hand along the keys in a familiar and intimate caress. It was as though the piano provided a repository for her emotions, she needed to touch it in order to know her own mind.

With her finger she lifted one of the keys. Along its side was an inscription, a small heart run through with an arrow, transposed between the initials A and D. She had carved these symbols herself, long ago. She let the key drop back into place and began to play.

As her fingers found the keys, releasing the melody, Ada closed her eyes, playing with heartfelt emotion, and the music filled Alisdair Stewart's house. Then, abruptly, she stopped, and turned to look over her left shoulder. There was no one sitting in the half-light, no one listening to her play. She tried to begin again, she tried to fill the emptiness that hollowed her soul, but, working the ivory keys with one hand, she could not continue. She stopped, disquieted, unable to go on, unable to get up, one hand on the lid and one on the piano keys. Ada McGrath had reached a dark place in her life; here was a turning that had to be negotiated somehow.

After some time had passed, how long she did not know, Flora burst in through the door, wanting Ada to come and look at the chickens. Galvanized, Ada picked up her cloak and bonnet: She would go to George Baines. She left the house immediately, telling Flora she must stay behind. She hurried along the narrow path, the wind once again whipping the bush into a frenzy of movement. Flora tagged along, full of dread at being left behind. The little girl clutched Ada's skirt with her fists, pulling her back and shouting, "Wait! Wait!" as though she knew where, and to what, Ada was headed.

Ada turned on Flora, snatching the skirt from her

hands and signing: "Go back. Don't you dare follow me!" The birds sang in the trees around them. Nothing that happened in this land seemed to disturb the birds from their songmaking.

"Why? Why can't I?" insisted Flora.

"Go and do your lessons," signed Ada.

In the near distance, Stewart made his way through the bush with Tahu, whom he had hired for the day. Hearing the shouting, he stopped and saw Ada leave Flora, who yelled, "I shan't practice and I DON'T CARE!" He could see them quite clearly.

Ada did not wait to listen to her daughter's complaints. Flora stamped back through the bush toward Stewart, her fists striking the air as she muttered, "Blast and damn. Bugger her! Bloody, bloody bugger her! I hope she falls face down in boiling mud! I hope wild dogs bite her 'til she bleeds! Bloody, bloody . . ."

Stewart emerged from the undergrowth in front of Flora, startling her. She looked up, her eyes wide with fright. "Where's your mother?" asked Stewart. "Where's she gone?"

Anger contorting her sweet face, Flora shouted: "TO HELL!" and hurtled off through the bush as fast as she could, expecting to be pursued for her wickedness.

Stewart clambered up the path where he had seen Ada disappear, catching glimpses of her distant figure, skirts flying as she hurried along. The wind was bothering the tops of the trees, setting them groaning, rubbing their branches against each other. Stewart followed, his wife ignorant of his pursuit.

Breathless, Ada swept through the door of Baines' hut without knocking. Baines was lying on his bed, sunk in torpor. He sat up. Ada stood by the door, unable to move any farther. Baines came toward her, blinking drowsiness away, aloof and perhaps a little suspicious. "So what brings you here?" he asked casually. Ada made no gesture, her expression did not alter. "Did you leave something?" Baines began to tuck in his shirt. "I have not found anything."

Still Ada did not move. Her look had a new vulnerability and openness that took Baines off his guard. "Does he know something?"

Ada shook her head and walked toward where the piano had once stood. She held herself in the empty space, looking around as though searching for a clue. The room felt heavy, the smell of the damp and mossy trees outside permeating the air.

"The piano was not harmed? It arrived safely?" Ada nodded. Neither knew what they wanted to happen next.

"Would you like to sit?" he asked. "I am going to sit." And he sat in his chair and took a drink from a glass set on a low table before him.

Ada did not sit. She stood immobilized. She sensed a great seriousness in Baines that moved her heart. He looked at her, searching for words, unmanned by her unexpected arrival and, more, by her strange, unwonted fragility.

"Ada," Baines said as though admonishing her. "Ada, I am unhappy." Here he paused. "Because I want you. Because my mind is seized on you and I can think of nothing else. This is how I suffer," he said, spreading his hands and smiling suddenly, defenseless. "I am sick with longing, I don't eat, I don't sleep." He looked up at her and it was clear to Ada that he was suffering. "So, if you've come with no feeling for me, then go." Saying this cost George Baines an enormous effort. Imagining he saw no response on Ada's face, his own face hardened. "Go," he said, indicating the door with a tilt of his head. "Go. Go." He stood and went toward the door, opening it for her himself.

Still Ada did not move, Baines' confession had pierced and immobilized her. She had never heard words like these. Her body was trembling and her chest burned, so she felt she must breathe very slowly or she might burst into flame. Why couldn't he see what she felt? Why was he telling her to go? She hated him for his blindness, for what he had done to her, for the possession he had taken of her body week by week. He had taught her body new senses, new desires, so that it no longer was her own. And now it had marched itself up to his hut against all she knew: her pride, her will, even her daughter.

But Baines could not see what was happening to Ada. He was convinced that she was playing with him casually, without feeling, and it angered him. "Go on. Get out," he spoke thickly with emotion. "Leave!" he shouted.

Stung by his words, Ada stepped toward him and, eyes filling with tears of anger, hit him hard across the face. Baines looked at her, shaken. Then Ada began to hit him again and again, slapping his face and shoulders. As Baines raised his arms to protect himself from her blows, his face began to open and glow as if she had spoken words of love. Ada was flushed and shocked; at this moment, face to face, they were profoundly aware of each other, profoundly equal. With each breath, with every second their eyes remained locked together, the promise of intimacy was confirmed and detailed until, like sleepwalkers who do not know how they come to be where they waken, George enfolded Ada in his arms. She trembled and tears spilled from her eyes. George lowered his head to softly kiss Ada's neck, then he moved his face upward until their lips met and they kissed and touched, lips, cheeks, noses, eyes, hair. There was nothing practiced about their tenderness, their emotions guided their instincts. George's face was full of the exquisite pain of his pleasure; Ada held him as though afraid he might disappear. They began to struggle with each other's clothes, anxious to touch more of one another's skin, lost to the world.

OUTSIDE, Alisdair Stewart surveyed George Baines' hut suspiciously, dropping his work bag by the stairs, heedless of Flynn's bark. Moving closer, he heard a deep sigh come from within the rough building. Without a thought, he knew not to knock at the door. Stewart stepped around the side of the hut stealthily, taking off his hat. Quaking, he peered through a space between the siding boards. Inside he saw George Baines and his wife, Ada McGrath.

$\mathcal{G}$EORGE and Ada pulled hard at the ribbons and lace of her clothing, buttons flying off, fasteners popping open, stays springing free. They kissed again, and that kiss let loose another wave of desire; an enormous urgency took hold of them, a delirium that neither had felt ever before. Fumbling with Ada's jacket, George fell to his knees and lifted her petticoat and hoops, burying his head in her scent. Ada's eyes closed, she sighed and moaned softly. George pulled her stockings down slowly; his large hands warm on her skin. With each touch their fever rose.

$\mathcal{S}$TEWART's lungs heaved and his mind raced. He reeled back from his peephole, still hearing the muted sighs of the man and woman within. Crushed and inflated with anger, not thinking clearly, he stepped up to look again instead of bursting through the door and throwing them apart. That fatal second look, the look for curiosity, was his undoing: He was transfixed, fettered, alone.

$\mathcal{A}$ D A lifted her skirt over her shoulders. As she removed each garment her bared skin felt electrified as it met the smooth, caressing air. She put her hands into George's hair as he knelt before her. She was smiling as she felt George's rough face against the skin of her thigh, his lips and tongue searching for her sweetness. She pulled him nearer; all the strange sensations were threatening to overwhelm her. Her face radiant, she shook with a pleasure so fierce she feared she might fall.

$\mathcal{S}$ T E W A R T leaned into the wall of the hut, a prisoner of his curiosity. He did not notice as the dog Flynn began to lick his hand. He could see that Baines had pulled down Ada's pantaloons and he could see her legs were bare. Suddenly, Stewart pulled his hand away from the dog and looked at it uncomprehendingly; it was wet with saliva. He wiped it on the boards and continued to watch, unable to move or act.

$\mathcal{I}$ N S I D E George's small room the raw, dark floorboards and walls contrasted with the soft whiteness of George and Ada's bodies. Cradling her slight body in his arms, he carried her across the room, laying her on his bed. It was dark in the hut, their way was lit by light seeping through the cracks and spaces between the wood siding. They were breathing in tandem, both in thrall to a sensual enchantment. Ada felt outside and inside herself at the same time, as though she were hallucinating, suffused with ecstasy, exalted by the enormous release she felt given with each embrace. Long black strands of her loosened hair stuck to her cheek and wrapped around her neck. Her cheeks were flushed and her eyes bright as George rolled his face across her breasts, gently, slowly, savoring the honeyed flavor of her body. She caressed his broad back, holding his body tightly to hers, and they continued as though drunk with bliss, rolling together as though rocked by waves. As they kissed, Ada's breath turned to low murmurs, small sounds that George found extraordinarily moving, causing him near to swoon with emotion. "What?" he asked Ada softly. "What? . . . Whisper."

ALISDAIR STEWART could not move, pinioned by his wife's luminous beauty and by the bodily enactment of love, which he had never known or witnessed.

As he lay over her now, the weight of George's body was sweet to Ada. They moved as one, possessed by the same spirit, their love a deep and dreadful joy. In the soft light, George's body seemed as large as Ada's was small, as square and knotted as she was curved and smooth, and he was afraid he might crush her, but she pulled him to her in a strong, uninhibited embrace full of passion and desire. And so they continued, skin

upon skin, bodies close and closer, falling into blessed-
ness. They made love many times, at first mindlessly,
urgently spilling their love into each other. His penis
and her vagina became all that there was of them, they
became their sex from the wildest thrusting to the most
exquisite stillness, until, exhausted, their lovemaking became slow like a long, endless kiss. Baines' heart opened
as he wept and laughed, feeling a love and awe for this
delicate feminine creature, who could so unman and
enthral him.

GEORGE sat on his bed, watching as Ada dressed. He
was unhappy and thoughtful in the cold aftermath of
their tenderness, wishing their idyll would never end.
"Now you are going I am miserable. Why's that?" Ada
moved closer to him so he could help do the buttons on
her sleeves, a small and familiar gesture that made his
heart expand further still. "Ada, I need to know, what
will you do? Will you come again?"

Ada picked up her jacket and began to collect the
missing buttons. She was distracted by certain reality,
worried by the time that had passed, concerned to get
dressed and return to Flora. She did not want to hear
George's questions; she had no answers for him. As she
reached to retrieve the last button she knocked it between
the loose wooden floor slats.

THE button fell through to where Alisdair Stewart had wedged himself under Baines' hut, down in the dark, musty space where Flynn hid from Flora, his tormentor. The button fell onto Stewart's neck, just missing his face, rolling down inside his shirt collar. He stifled a gasp, not wanting to betray his presence.

"WAIT," said George. "I don't know what you are thinking." Ada quickly tidied her hair, pinning the looping plaits where they had tumbled free, drawing herself back down to solid ground. "Does this mean something to you?" George asked softly. "I already miss you. Ada," he reached one arm to her waist, "do you love me?"

Ada stilled, considering this question, looking in the mirror at her face, which was not changed or marked, although she half expected it to be. She felt she did not know how to reply. What did she feel, except a complex pleasure, except a dark kind of secret awakening? Ada turned to George slowly and then lifted his shirt, kissing his chest as though she might devour him instead of answering. George felt confused—this was an answer, was it not?—yet he felt absent in her exploring of him. He pulled his lover away so that he might study her face. "Come tomorrow," he said urgently. "If the answer is yes, come tomorrow." Ada resumed kissing George, as if she could not get enough of the taste of his skin, as if she had not tasted skin before.

Chapter 9

THINKING her secret safe, Ada was elated and free of care that night. As they prepared for sleep, she allowed Flora to brush her hair. But instead of sitting patiently as she would on any other evening, Ada jumped up and began to spin around and around the room in secret rapture, smiling and laughing soundlessly, while Flora, standing on the bed, laughed and shrieked, "Mother, stay still!"

In the next room Stewart listened to their noise and giggles, his jaw clenched, his neck stiff and unbending. His hair was wet and neatly combed from his bath, and he sat brooding over a journal of pressed botanical specimens that he had collected over the years, not looking at the pages. After a few moments, he stood and walked toward the door of the bedroom where Flora and Ada tumbled on the bed, their long dark hair and white nightdresses rendering them almost indistinguishable from one another, two small joyous figures. Stewart's fury was barely containable, he was frightened by it; what could he

say to his wife now? Ada's silence seemed to silence him
as well. He left them to their play, and went outside to
chop wood in the dark until he saw the lamp in their bedroom expire.

$\mathcal{T}$HE next day, when Ada saw Stewart depart for his endless task of fencing the perimeter of his land, she hastened from the house, without disturbing Flora at play.
Quickly, she ran down the path to George's hut, her heart
brimming. The sky was dark and the treetops were sway-
ing furiously. The forest seemed suddenly malevolent
and without end.

Ada, out of breath, glanced behind as if to guard
against followers—she was thinking of Flora—when directly in front of her Alisdair Stewart materialized on the
path. Ada stopped short. The look on his face was unlike
any expression she had yet seen. His eyes did not look at
her but all about her, in a way more animal than human,
enraged, wounded, and uncomprehending. He knew
where she was heading, and she read in his face that
somehow he knew what had transpired there the previous
day. She lowered her eyes and walked steadily past her
husband, then continued along the path as though he had
not intercepted her, hurrying with straight-backed dignity and set face. But he followed right behind, catching
her up and grabbing her by one arm and then pulling her
to him, kissing her fiercely, arms wrapped tightly around
her. Ada struggled and pushed, slipping downward, out

and away as his grip faltered. She ran, but she could not escape him, and the hoary bush offered no relief. Stewart seized her again and dragged her away from the tree that she had clasped in desperation, he mercilessly pulling her with all his strength, she clinging to the branch with all of hers, until she could cling no longer. He pushed her down into the leaves and the mud, and threw himself upon her, his face, red and roughened, pressed close to hers, which was cold and utterly drained of color. Their eyes met and, in that moment of hesitation, Ada managed to push Stewart away again. She tried to sit up but he lifted her dress, forcing his hand violently between her legs, tearing at her undergarments. Ada groaned, turning herself this way and that, back and forth, shoving and kicking her husband, dragging down her skirt, pushing his hands away from where they touched her. Ada crawled through the undergrowth while Stewart clung to her skirt, pulling her toward him, hand over hand like a sailor hauling in an anchor. The thick supplejack vines were like many arms that reached out to bind her, gray snakes coiling around her, a terrible web itself in league with the man who had brought her to this place.

Then he was upon her again, his large hands around her waist.

"Mumma, Mumma!" cried Flora, coming into distant view. Distraught and in tears, her angel wings twisted about her, Flora shouted, "They are playing your piano."

At the sound of the child's voice, Stewart relinquished his grip on Ada, allowing her to get free. She brushed off her skirt and gave him a look of such reproach that for a moment he felt it was he who had sinned, and he hung his head low with odium. Ada gathered her shredded composure and went toward the child.

In Stewart's house a group of Maoris were stationed around the piano. Chief Nihe's daughter was attempting to play the instrument, banging out loud, discordant sound.

Flora followed Ada, who was clutching her bonnet and straightening her skirt, back to the house. But by the time they arrived the Maoris were leaving.

Stewart followed his wife down the hill. Without pausing to speak to her or Flora, he went straight to the woodpile and began to cut up lengths of board. Ada sat in the bedroom, shivering and covering her ears, afraid of what she had set in motion. Stewart commenced hammering, nailing the planks over the windows, shutting out what little light there was. Flora, her angel wings drooping, gave Stewart directions from inside the house, joining in the spirit of the exercise. "Here, Papa," she said, her hands on the window indicating where he had left a gap. She had begun to call him papa almost without noticing. She looked to her mother for a reaction, but, as had become customary, Ada paid no heed.

All the rest of that day, Ada lay on the bed, examining her face in her hand mirror, still looking for a change or a sign. George's face was marked, why not hers now? She rolled onto one side and touched her cheek, staring into the mirror. Slowly, she brought the mirror toward herself and gave her reflection a lingering kiss in a movement that was sensual and strange.

His work went quickly until, on the veranda, Stewart lowered a wooden bolt over the outside of the front door, imprisoning Ada within.

$\mathcal{L}$ATER, Flora approached the bed where her mother lay. "You shouldn't have gone up there, should you," she scolded. She came round the side of the bed and sat down. "I don't like it and nor does Papa." Opening her box she reached in and drew out a deck of playing cards. Dealing the cards one at a time onto Ada's hip, she said, "We can play cards though, if you like." But Ada rolled away, her eyes closed, pressing her face and body into the mattress, as if for comfort. Flora looked on, her child's face suddenly adult with strain and confusion, as the cards fell to the bed, untouched.

$\mathcal{A}$ND so they were locked in, barred into the house as though it were a jail. Stewart had decided to teach Ada a lesson, and it was a bitter school in which she would learn. The boards had gone up, one after the other, and with each nail Ada forced herself further away from the present, deeper inside, down a long corridor of memory.

*A*DA MCGRATH did not see Delwar Haussler for one week after their embrace. It took her seven days before she regained her confidence, before she felt she would not be betrayed by her blushes. She had no idea what he thought of her, she was not about to give away how she felt about him.

Delwar Haussler did not attempt to seek Ada out; he knew this was not appropriate to his station, and he worried that pursuing her might drive her away. When she had got up and left the room that evening the previous week, he had watched her go without speaking. That kiss had caused a transformation within; when he looked at Ada he no longer saw a child. He saw her for herself, what she was, not what she seemed. He thought her extraordinary.

The music room lay dormant for seven days. During that time Wyston McGrath did not notice anything amiss. One afternoon he passed by the room and saw that Delwar and Ada were not there, but as soon as he moved away from the open door his mind was absorbed by other thoughts once more. Beadsley, the lawyer, had issued a stern administrative warning to McGrath earlier that week. "You must put your affairs in order, before it is too late," he had said ominously. Wyston had sighed heavily before suggesting, in a voice laden with familiar irony, that this was the very reason for which he retained a lawyer and an accountant.

Ada spent most of the week in her room. Household staff who inquired after her were sent away in an imperious manner more suited to a child than the young woman Ada felt she had suddenly become. Bored within a few hours of her first day of self-imposed exile, Ada took up her loathed needlework. She would finish this sampler for her father; perhaps she would make something for Delwar as well.

But soon the needle and cloth were pushed to one side. Ada was more comfortable lying on the bed, staring out the open window, and dreaming, romancing herself and Delwar Haussler, no other thought in her mind.

After the week had passed, Ada felt her composure regained and, at the usual time, she made her way to the music room. Delwar sat in a chair next to the piano, as had been his practice for a few hours at this time every day that week. He had not been out at all in the evenings, avoiding his friends, avoiding music even. He had been most concerned to avoid Judith McDougall, whose considerable charms had paled and faded in his mind.

Delwar stood clumsily when he realized that Ada had entered the room. She smiled, politely, a little coolly. He, flustered, moved forward to take her hand, and then thought better of it. She nodded formally, and indicated that she wanted him to play for her.

Delwar performed badly that afternoon, his fingers stumbling, slurring the notes. Ada had never heard him play like this, he was usually such a careful technician, but if she was surprised, she did not show it. However, she was secretly flattered by his discomfort, and she did notice how pink his neck and cheeks had become. She brushed her hand against her own cheek, which remained cool.

Delwar asked Ada to play, but she refused. He longed to speak to her, to ask how she felt, to apologize for his forthrightness, to pass his own hand across her cheek. But he did nothing except play brisk Chopin. After an hour, he could stand the tension no longer. He knew he had to do something: either throw himself upon her, or leave the room. He stood, bumping against the piano bench. Then he left the room without speaking.

Ada watched from the window of the music room while Delwar stalked across the lawn, toward the stream. She sat down and played the piano when she was sure he would hear no echo of her chords. She improvised, taking what she had learned from Delwar and making the piano sing, giving voice to all her thoughts and feelings.

Every afternoon Delwar and Ada met in the music room as before. For the first month, Delwar played and Ada listened. His playing did not improve, for his mind was on a twisting and turning course, never calm with the music, never at ease. He moved from despair to elation, from action to passivity, from longing to loneliness within one four/four phrase. Some days the music notes danced on the staff paper before his eyes; he could not read the music, the music would not let itself be read. So then he attempted to play from memory. Unlike Ada, he was not a pianist who improvised.

Then, one afternoon, Ada consented to play herself. She sat down and began, without music, a composition that Delwar had not heard before. "What is this?" he asked, when she finished. "Which composer is this?" Embarrassed by his ignorance, he was eager to know. Had Ada been practicing when he was not there?

But of course, Ada would give no answer. She left her silver notecase dangling from her neck and continued playing. The piece was of her own composition. It had come into her head during the night, and today she played it unexpurgated. But she felt too shy to admit this to Delwar. She took pleasure in his scholarly consternation. As she played he sat back down and listened.

Their afternoons resumed the old pattern. Delwar gave instruction, he played examples, Ada watched and followed his leads. They had become very formal with each other once more, polite and obsequious, mindful of each other like the early days. Delwar was desperate to break down the barrier that he felt rising between them. Ada knew he was distracted, but what he wanted, she could not give.

Ada did not think of marrying Delwar Haussler, as prior to their embrace she had not thought of marrying anyone. She was not worried about her father's opinion of Delwar, of herself even; she was not concerned with what anyone might think. But she did not want to lose herself to a situation where control might not be regained. She wanted things to be as they had been, before Miss McDougall, before that night, when the world consisted of herself and Delwar and the piano.

This was what she told herself she wanted, keeping

strict counsel, but of course she wanted other things as well. At night she dreamt of his arms around her, at night she dreamt of Delwar's warm lips; she could not control what visions came to her in her slumber.

At times Delwar felt he had lapsed into madness. Was the embrace just a fantasy, an illusion, something he had concocted? His friends came to call and attempted to arouse his enthusiasm for concerts and recitals and performances again, but he did not respond to their remonstrations. He took himself for long walks in the mornings, while he waited for the afternoon to arrive. He wrote letters to Ada that he did not post; he made speeches that she would never hear.

And yet Delwar was not a practical man, indeed he was the opposite, a romantic. He did not spend his days scheming how one day Ada would belong—betrothed—to him. He did not rehearse representations to Wyston McGrath, he did not ask for money from his sisters to set up house. Like Ada, he did not think of marriage. She was his pupil, he was her tutor. That gulf could not be bridged. The relationship was immutable.

And then a strategy occurred to Delwar. He ordered new sheet music by post from London, handing the invoice to Wyston when the material finally arrived one clear morning. He took the freshly printed pages to the piano and paced the room, waiting for Ada to appear.

"Well, Ada," he said when she entered the music room, looking as calm and self-contained as always. "I have some new music for you to learn. It is a piece called

'Fantasia in F Minor' by Schubert." Ada looked at him inquiringly. Delwar often brought new music to her piano, but seldom made such a display of his enterprise. She sat at the piano bench, and he spread the sheets before her with a flourish. Ada stared at the staff lines. The notes were laid out in a manner to which she was unaccustomed. She thought she had learned how to read music, and she was proud of her increasing grasp of theory. But this was something quite different.

"It's a duet!" Delwar announced triumphantly. Ada looked up at him, her expression changing, her eyes widening. "It is written for four hands. Four hands on one piano." Ada looked back down at the notes, which swam into sensible formation. "Wonderful, isn't it," he continued, brimming with pleasure over his conceit. "And you are going to learn to play it with me. It is a challenge that most good pianists should be made to undertake, you make a better—richer—music this way."

At that Delwar moved toward the piano bench. He sat down; the bench was only just large enough to contain them both. Ada moved as far as she could to one side, but as she created space Delwar seemed to fill it, his right arm and leg pressing against her left. She could not move any farther and still be able to play. She stood and fetched a chair, but Delwar had thought of that. "Too low," he announced, patting the space beside him, "we'd be too far apart—you couldn't reach all the keys."

And so Ada sat beside Delwar, and she endured his capricious tutelage, thinking of little else apart from his thigh pressed against hers. When he moved his foot on the pedals, the whole length of his leg seemed to move against hers. She felt herself flush; she fought to retain her composure.

The first piece was pleasing, like many duets rather wistful and romantically otherworldly, calculated to produce a volume of sound unattainable by solo players. They both played slowly at first, unfamiliar with each other's rhythms. It was necessary to employ the metronome to keep time. As the hours passed, Delwar produced more duets, a new one every day for a week, marches, waltzes, symphonies by Beethoven and Mozart transcribed for four hands, until they seemed to play nothing else. The household staff caught wind of what was happening; there was much giggling and peeking at the pair at their music. But the sounds they produced were full and sweet enough, and Wyston McGrath admired the tutor and his pupil for their musical compatibility.

At first Ada was infuriated by what she thought of as Delwar Haussler's ruse. The instrument was not meant for two players; it was ridiculous. She had always enjoyed the solipsism the piano afforded. But then she loved music so, and this was a new challenge and, without really trying, she knew she would be unable to resist. Some of the melodies were quite lovely. After a while she began to lose herself to the music again. And the sensation of playing, giving all, at the same time as someone else, was exquisite. Four hands did make a full, harmonious noise that two hands could not, just as Delwar had said. Ada felt her resolve disappear, dissolving like salts in a hot bath giving way to luxury. She felt close to Delwar Haussler, brought near through music and now nearer through the frequent proximity of their bodies. She felt as though a whole new world had been revealed to her; she claimed a rare and odd curiosity, and she had no fear. She was a strange girl, out of her time, but Delwar did not see that. He saw a small, soft, young woman with dark, expressive eyes and an unusual passion for the piano.

One night Ada stole down to the music room long after the household had retired. She reached under the piano lid and drew an ivory key from the keyboard. Then she sat with the needle and candle she had carried from her room and carved a girlish approximation of her feelings into the side of the key which, when complete, she replaced in the keyboard carefully. Ada felt at one with Delwar; sometimes she imagined he could read her thoughts. In a sense he could read Ada's mind, although that sense was musical and nothing as remarkable or entire as Ada's dreamy imaginings would have it.

And then, on Christmas Eve, several months later, Delwar Haussler and the McGrath household were invited to a special concert in Aberdeen. After some deliberation Delwar decided he would like to attend, and he asked Ada and her father to accompany him. Ada was reluctant, not wanting to watch Delwar among his friends after so long of having him to herself, but Wyston consented and Ada felt she must also take part. Her father had not been well lately, and she hoped an evening out would cheer him. And, of course, she did not really want Delwar to attend without her.

But, when Christmas Eve arrived, Wyston was not well enough to go out, and he retired before dinner, hoping to conserve his energy. So Ada and Delwar went unchaperoned, with her father's blessing.

The music was lovely and the event well attended; it seemed most of Aberdeen was there. When it finished, Delwar and Ada left almost immediately. Delwar did not mention anything to Ada, but he did not want to be swamped by his friends, he wanted to get away in the cold night air where he could walk with Ada on his arm. They slipped away, down the icy cobbled streets, before anyone could intercept them.

At the house, all was quiet. Wyston was sleeping in his chamber at the back of the house. The staff had been given the evening off to be with their families. In the entrance hall Delwar made as though to wish Ada goodnight, but before he spoke she took his arm and led him up to the music room. Shuffling through the stacks of sheet music, Ada handed Delwar a sheaf that he knew was her favorite, and indicated that she would like him to play for her.

Ada sat in the chair beside the piano, closed her eyes and waited for Delwar to begin. In the lamplight, she looked beautiful, her face still, her pale skin gilded by the light reflecting off the windows, the Christmas decorations and the piano's polished rosewood. Delwar looked at her for a long moment, and then he began to play.

The music transported Ada into another world where everything had the texture of silk and all was warmth and small rooms made cozy by hearthfires at night. The music made her heart sing, it made her breath quicken, it filled her with longing for something she could not have expressed.

Delwar watched her as he played. When he finished, she opened her eyes and smiled. "It's my turn to choose," he said. And he picked the longest, most emotive of the duets that they had learned together recently.

Ada took her place on the bench beside Delwar. When she sat down, he took a deep breath and her scent filled his thoughts. They began to play. They played the piece once, and they played it perfectly, with a rhythm, a strength, a feeling they had not previously discovered. At the end they sat in silence, the piano music still reverberating around the room. And then they turned to each other, to one another's arms. They stood, still embracing, and with one foot Delwar pushed the piano bench away.

In the house of Alisdair Stewart, Ada walked in her sleep. Disturbing Flora, who followed her out of the bedroom, she went toward the piano, sat down, and began to play. Her hair was loose and tumbling down her back, and her nightdress seemed thin, insubstantial. The music was insistent, loud, and strong, the same progression of chords over and over, a tense piece, discordant, without real melody. She played without ceasing, head bowed low, shoulders bent, hardly seeming to breathe, her hands as confident on the keyboard as they were when she was awake.

The music roused Stewart, who climbed out of bed to find Ada playing and Flora standing at her side. He carried a candlelamp into the parlor.

"She's asleep. Look," Flora said passing her hand in front of Ada's face, as though her mother were blind. Ada played on, the music slightly calmer now, as if in her sleep she was reassured by Flora's voice. "One night," Flora said to Stewart, her voice low and intoxicated with the story, "she was found in her nightgown on the road to London. Grandfather said her feet were cut so badly she couldn't walk for a week."

Stewart placed the lamp on the piano, leaning over so that he could examine the shuttered visage of his somnambulant wife, thinking her sleeping state might explain her waking behavior. The two watched Ada, hypnotized by her compulsive recital, until all at once her fingers stilled, she rose up and stared, as if she had seen a phantom, before allowing herself to be led back to bed by her daughter.

Later, returned to bed, Ada dreamed of George. She dreamed of herself in George's arms, his kisses, caresses. In her dream, she rolled toward him, placing her hand on his back, burying her face in his skin. She heard George moan, she felt him move toward her.

Suddenly Ada awoke. With a shock, she realized that the body she caressed so tenderly was Flora's. Struck by a sudden impulse, she rose from her bed and walked into the bedroom of her husband.

Ada sat beside the supine form of Alisdair Stewart without waking him. He had gone to sleep with his lamp still lit, and the room was suffused with a dim, soft yellow light. She had not witnessed him sleeping before, and Ada thought Stewart looked peaceful, more at ease asleep than awake. She reached out and her hand hovered above him before she touched his cheek, stroking his skin, smooth, then whiskered, then smooth again. Stewart awoke, opening his eyes. He looked toward his wife, anxious and surprised by her unprecedented arrival at his bedside, but as Ada continued to move her hand down his neck, circling her hand around his throat, stroking his collarbone, then pushing her hand slowly under his nightshirt to touch the warm skin there, he whispered her name, "Ada." Then he closed his eyes again.

What was she doing here with him on this evening, after all he had witnessed at George Baines' hut? Ada McGrath would never fail to confound Alisdair Stewart; she did not react, she did not seem to think, like the few other women whom he knew. She was a different sort of creature altogether, hardly human he sometimes thought. Alisdair felt himself shunted between conflicting emotions as his wife touched him. He wanted her to continue, he wanted what George Baines had been given, but he was appalled and attracted at the same time.

Ada McGrath did not know why she had felt drawn to her husband's bedside on that night. Trapped in the house as she was—no exit, and no entrance either without Stewart's permission—she had to make some kind of movement to still what she felt stirring inside, a directionless longing, a hunger begun with George Baines for the touch of skin upon skin.

Stewart closed his eyes again, trying not to break the spell. Ada rolled down the sheet that covered his body, then she lifted his shirt smoothly, exposing his stomach and chest to the night air. Stewart drew his breath. She ran her hands over his chest, avoiding his eyes, her own face rapt, as though her desire had been wakened and now could not sleep until it had been explored in some way.

Stewart's eyes welled with tears and he looked up at Ada's face like a child after a bad dream, fearful and trusting. Ada continued to touch him like a faith healer spreading balm on a wound; tenderly and attentively she stroked down toward his belly. Stewart's skin goosebumped and he shuddered. He could bear the tension no longer. He reached out for his wife, lifting himself out of the bed toward her. But she sprang back, frowning, disappointed somehow. Then she left Alisdair Stewart's bedroom, returning to her own without giving any indication of her thoughts or feelings.

$\mathcal{W}$HEN Aunt Morag and Nessie arrived for a visit, trailing Heni and Mary in their wake, they were horrified by the fortified state of their nephew's house. Ada and Flora sat at the kitchen table playing a desultory game of cards, withering like plants deprived of sunlight. Alisdair Stewart had not permitted them to leave the house that morning.

"Alisdair, is it because of our play?" asked Morag anxiously. "Have the natives aggressed you?" Stewart was carrying some logs to the fire, determined to get on with the day. Morag continued, walking over to the door, "I have to say you have done the wrong thing here." She pointed: "You have put the latch on the outside you see. Now when you close the door," she closed it, "it will be the Maoris that lock *you* in, you see? With the latch on that side you are quite trapped."

Nessie nodded her head seriously, ". . . quite trapped."

While Morag spoke, Heni and Mary sat in a corner investigating one of Flora's dolls. Absorbed, they ignored the *pakeha* and their peculiar talk. Stewart stood behind Ada and Flora silently, allowing Morag to indulge her fantasies.

Morag continued to speak as she came over to the table and began to unwrap the basket full of clothes and packets of food that she had brought as gifts to the household. "We have just come from George Baines, and they have taken him over." At this Ada looked up, listening. Her hair was not as tightly plaited as was her custom, in fact Morag thought she looked in disarray. "It is no wonder he is leaving, he has got in too deep with the natives. They sit on his floor as proud as kings, but without a shred of manners."

". . . shred of manners," chanted Nessie.

"He is quite altered," said Morag, "as if they had been trying some native witchcraft on him. Well, tomorrow or the day after, he'll be gone." Morag unwrapped biscuits and petite cakes and began to place them on plates on the table.

Ada, her face expressionless but suddenly very pale, rose and walked toward the piano.

"So Baines is packing up," said Stewart gruffly, his words conveying layers of meaning to Ada as she crossed the room.

"Well, he has nothing to pack, but he is leaving." As Morag spoke, Nessie picked up a handkerchief and began to snivel. "And it is just as well," Aunt Morag continued. "Nessie has foolishly grown an affection for him . . . we have had some tears." Nessie's face crumpled on cue and she began to sob. Morag spoke firmly to her young companion. "Stop it." Nessie sobbed. "Stop. STOP!" Nessie, remarkably, obeyed the edict, blinking her face back into shape.

Ada moved silently and steadily toward the piano, hoping to still her emotions and disguise her agitation. As she began to play, Morag said to Stewart, "I am quite frightened of the way back, we must leave in good light. Will we be safe?"

At first Ada's playing faltered, but she quickly became absorbed. The piano took her away from the claustrophobic parlor. The music took her to George Baines.

Stewart reassured Morag, hoping that his aunt and her companions would leave. "Oh yes, if you leave now I am sure of it."

They paused, momentarily, to listen to Ada's playing. She was bent over the piano, fully within the music, blocking out everything else. They all stared, intrigued with the melody and Ada's singular concentration. By now they were accustomed to Ada's unorthodox habits, although her behavior never failed to amaze them. As Stewart watched his wife he thought of what had passed during the night, and felt only confusion and longing.

ON their journey home, Aunt Morag could talk of nothing but the strange tableau they had witnessed at her nephew's house. "Alisdair is most changed since their arrival, most changed." She shook her head thoughtfully. Ada McGrath was not like other young, newly emigrated wives. She was too unusual, that was a fact. Her muteness, her piano playing, and, of course, the child. For all her Christian charity, Aunt Morag still wondered about the wisdom of her nephew marrying a woman whose first child was not his, fatherless in the eyes of the Lord. She had expected his sacrifice to ennoble Alisdair, but the whole family seemed miserable indeed.

Midway along the path, Aunt Morag decided she

must attempt a discreet stop. Nessie, Heni, and Mary kept guard, holding up blankets and capes to afford Morag a little privacy. It was a windy day and the blankets billowed. While she squatted low to ground, her skirts puffed around her, Aunt Morag ruminated. "You know, I am thinking of the piano. She does not play the piano as we do Nessie."

The blankets had begun to droop as the girls listened. "Up!" hissed Morag before continuing. "No, she is a strange creature and her playing is strange, like a mood that passes into you." Again the blankets drooped. "Up! Now your playing, Nessie, is plain and true and that is what I like." Nessie nodded and smiled. "To have a sound creep inside you is not at all pleasant."

Just then there was a loud fluttering in the bush. "What's that?" whispered Morag.

Nessie, looking overhead gave a shriek. Not waiting for Aunt Morag to finish collecting herself, Nessie gathered her blanket and rushed off.

"It's a pigeon, Auntie," reassured Heni calmly.

"Oh," said Aunt Morag, hurrying after Nessie, dismayed. "I should have waited."

STEWART was not asleep as Ada McGrath entered his bedroom that night. "I waited for you," he murmured. The light from her lamp produced a warm glow. Ada began to caress her husband's neck, smoothing his hair away from his forehead where it rested on the pillow. His face was pleasant to look on. She stroked him lightly, her mind now blank but for the sensation in her fingertips. Stewart's muscles tensed as he tried to lie still, not wanting to startle her and perhaps cause her to leave. Ada pushed his shirt upward and stroked her husband's back, her direct tenderness both painful and enticing to Stewart. After a moment he felt her gently ease his undergarments down, exposing his buttocks. He held his breath, stunned and aroused by her immodesty, while she caressed the cheek in a soft, circling movement, like she might soothe a baby. Stewart nervously grabbed his clothes, hauling them upward over his buttocks with clenched fists. Ada sat back for a moment, letting him relax, and then she began her experiment again, easing his hand away from where he gripped the cloth, lowering the garments in a methodical, self-absorbed way. And it was this that so disturbed her husband; she seemed to be touching him for her own pleasure.

Ada began to stroke Alisdair Stewart's buttocks again, moving her hand gently between the cheeks. Her touch bedeviled him; he felt vulnerable, helpless, hopeless even. Again, he was overwhelmed by a terrible mixture of anger, embarrassment, and lust. Yanking up his garments, he moved away from Ada, until he was sitting on the opposite side of the bed, his back to her. Ada calmly watched his retreat.

"I want to touch you," Stewart said, his voice low, his breath quick. "Why can't I touch you? Don't you like me?"

Ada looked at him across the bed as though from a great unbreachable distance. She pitied his helpless dolor, was moved by it even, but felt as though it had nothing to do with her.

A searing wave of disappointment and fiery shame coursed through Stewart's body as Ada McGrath rose to return to her own room.

Chapter *10*

ᘉ D A and Flora were woken by sunlight and the sound of Stewart ripping the boards from their window. He had risen from his troubled sleep with no stomach for keeping a woman and child prisoner, no matter how unhappy his marriage might be. Flora pulled on her angel wings and ran outside in her nightdress and Wellington boots, chasing the chickens, happy to be in the sun. The roosters crowed in confirmation while Ada dressed and put her hair into fresh plaits, pinning them into place.

Stewart came in after he had finished dismantling his fortifications. "We must get on," he said to Ada, lowering his head. "I've decided to trust you to stay here. You won't see Baines." This last was not quite a question, nor yet a command. He looked at Ada carefully, determined to view her nocturnal visits positively. Ada returned his gaze steadily, and shook her head. "Good," he said, sitting down beside her, "good." He paused. "Perhaps with time you might come to like me?" Ada did not look at Stewart then, did not indicate whether she agreed. She picked up her hand mirror to inspect her hair.

Stewart departed, carrying with him his fence-building equipment, taking enough food for the day. From the window, Ada watched him leave. As soon as he rounded the corner and was out of sight, she went to the piano. Opening the lid, she reached in to where the keys met the strings. Deftly, she lifted one ivory key away from the keyboard, pulling it out of its resting place. Then, seated at the table where she had carved a keyboard long weeks ago, she took a needle and, heating it in the flame of a candle in direct repetition of a scene she had enacted nearly ten years before, she engraved a phrase on one side of the key: "Dear George, you have my heart." Magical words for a man who could not read, sent by a woman who could not speak. She signed her carving, "Ada McGrath." Then she wrapped the precious cargo in a linen cloth, bound by a green silk ribbon. Ada believed with all her soul that George Baines would understand her message.

Taking the key, Ada went outside to where Flora was playing. The child had constructed a miniature clothesline, and she was washing her dolls' clothes in a bucket of cold water. While she worked she spoke aloud. "Keep quiet," she said to her dollies. "You'll just have to be naked while I am washing and drying your clothes." Ada approached her, kneeling down by her daughter and showing her the carefully wrapped parcel.

"Take this to Baines," Ada signed. "It belongs to him."

Flora shook her head, wary of her mother. "No, we're not supposed to visit him."

"You take it to him," Ada insisted. She would not break her own promise to Stewart, but he had not bound Flora with his request.

The child ignored her mother, returning to her washing. Ada pulled Flora to her feet with sudden violence. She placed the parcel firmly in Flora's hand and sent her on her way.

Upset and infuriated with her mother, Flora walked along the path humming aggressively. When she came to where it forked—left to Mr. Baines' hut, right to where Papa was working—she went a little distance toward Mr. Baines', then hesitated and took the right fork instead. She knew that she was making the correct choice. Papa had said they mustn't go to visit George Baines. Mumma was bad. She had done wrong, and they had both been punished. Mumma could not be obeyed. She wanted her mother to stay home and love her again. Something had happened up at George Baines' that had taken her mother from her. It seemed obvious that he was the source of their problems. Flora followed the path along Stewart's fence posts, up to the crest of a hill, then down its spine and up again. "The grand old Duke of York," she sang, skipping, ". . . he had ten thousand men, he marched them up to the top of the hill and he marched them down again."

The line of fence seemed endless as Flora trudged up yet another hill, but finally she could see Stewart working where the fence finished, halfway up the side of the next hill. ". . . And when they're up they're up, and when they're down they're down, and when they're only halfway up they're neither up nor down . . ." Stewart was driving in a new post, watched by Mana, Tahu, and another, none of whom were driven to help. Instead, they offered advice, which Stewart ignored. "Crooked, Mr Stewart," said Tahu of the post, "crooked." Stewart stopped hammering when Flora appeared, breathless and flushed.

"Mother wanted me to give this to Mr. Baines." Flora brandished the linen-covered piano key. "I thought maybe it was not a proper thing to do. Shall I open it?" She began to untie the ribbon.

"No, give it to me," said Stewart, leaning over to take the key from the girl. Suspicious of the parcel's contents, and uncomfortable with Flora watching, he slowly unwrapped it and, turning the key over, read the message inscribed on its side. A chill ran through his heart, and he felt a fire in the pit of his stomach. His breath came quickly and he staggered, clenching the key in his fist, looking up at the sky. In that instant the world made no sense. What in God's name was happening to him? The Maoris, who were seated on the ground relaxing, noticed that something was amiss; Tahu sat up to take a better look. Dropping the key and grabbing his axe, Stewart began to run down the hill. Mana called after him, but he did not reply. The young man stood, picking up the key.

"*Kaare e Waiata. Kaare e Waiata,*—It's lost its voice—it can't sing," he said.

Alisdair Stewart ran, seeing nothing, pursued by rage, led by jealousy. The day changed from sunshine to sudden darkness. It began to rain and a thunderstorm rumbled, brewing malignantly on the horizon. Flora followed, unaware of Stewart's anguish. He soon left her behind as he sped through the rain.

Ada looked up from her book as Stewart burst into the house, his wet hair splattered against his forehead, his face drained of color. She knew immediately what had happened. She sprang from the table as the axe embedded itself in the wood, chopping off the corner of the book she had been reading. Ada ran toward the wall. Stewart pulled the axe out of the table, his expression terrible, the tendons in his neck bulging. "Why? I trusted you," he said, his teeth clenched. He swung the axe again, this time aiming for the piano. It made a loud bass thudding noise as it wedged in the lid, and Ada threw herself at her husband in an attempt to save her piano. He turned, grabbing her by the shoulders. "I trusted you," he shouted, jerking her across the room, his voice vibrating. "I trusted you, do you hear?" He pushed her onto the table, still shaking her small body, sending spools of thread and cloth spinning. "Why do you make me hurt you?" Stewart pushed himself against Ada, pressing his lips to her cheek in a violent embrace. Then he lifted her from the table and rushed her backward until her body hit the wall. "We could be happy," he cried, slamming her against the hard partition once more. Ada sagged in his grip. She had no strength against the vehemence of his furious grasp. "You have made me angry! Speak!"

Then, taking the axe, he dragged Ada out of the house into the storm and the mud, past the now petrified Flora who was standing outside in the heavy rain. The sky was very low, the clouds dark with menace. "You shall answer for this," Stewart shouted, yanking Ada by the arm as she desperately held onto a sheet hanging from the clothesline. "Speak or not, you shall answer for it!" Flora watched, too frightened to intervene as Stewart dragged Ada through the mud, toward the woodchop. The rain came down relentlessly.

Ada saw where they were headed. She bucked and struggled, but Stewart was infinitely stronger than she. At the woodchop she broke free and crawled away through the splinters and mud. Axe in hand, Stewart was quick upon her again, grasping her by the neck of her dress, then her hair, pulling her backwards, his arm clamped tightly around her neck, toward the cutting block. There, he took her right hand and held it in place on the woodchop.

"Do you love him?" he shouted. "Do you? Is it him you love?" He raised the axe. Flora screamed, "She says: 'NO!' " but her words, if he heard them, did not give him pause. Stewart brought the axe down with all his might. Ada's muddied face stared into oblivion. She did not call

out or scream, she only grabbed Stewart's leg convul-
sively, gazing blankly as her daughter screamed. Blood
spurted, striking Flora's white pinafore, her angel wings
already covered in mud.

A moment passed—a dark moment of silence where
everyone and everything, even the birds, seemed utterly
silent—and then Ada's face buckled in pain. Stewart released her from his grasp. Ada stood, taking a few, falter-
ing steps away through the mud, and then turned to look
at what he had done, what was left on the woodchop. She
was pale, her hand pulsing blood as she clutched it, trying
to staunch the flow. She saw what he had done, her index
finger, cut clean through the bone, remained on the
block. She looked to the sky, wondering how she had
come to this place. Covered in mud and blood, Ada
turned, instinctively, toward George Baines' hut. Ada
kept moving, as if her life depended on it. Flora, still calling to her mother, trotted parallel to her. Her face ashen,
Ada walked unsteadily, without seeing, mustering all her
strength and dignity. She stumbled, fell to her knees,
both hands forward into the mud, indifferent to the pain,
then rose again. Finally, slowly, like a sinking ship, she
collapsed in the mire, her dress billowing around her as
she sank to the ground.

"Mother!" Flora screamed.

Stewart, heart still pounding in his ears, wrapped the
finger in a white handkerchief. He handed it to the child,
who backed away from him, terrified. "You give this to

Baines," he said, in a low, disembodied voice. "Tell him if he ever tries to see her again I'll take off another and another and another."

Flora began to run, pausing for a moment when she reached her mother. "Run!" shouted Stewart, and Flora flew down the path.

For the past several days Baines had waited, yearning, for Ada to return, but the long hours passed and slowly his joy faded, to be replaced by the bitter knowledge that she would not come. He could neither eat nor sleep and he could find no peace. He had to leave.

As part of his brief and sad farewell to this place where he had lived so happily and so long, George Baines traveled by horseback to the *Pa*, the Maori village. Hira met him at the entrance to the walled *Pa*, which stood on the edge of a broad slow-moving river. Mangrove trees hung down into the rich silted soil, and beyond the trees, canoes lined the flat. Hira said that everyone had come to bid Peini farewell. The *Pa* was long established, in a continual state of regeneration and repair, and although Baines had visited often, he always felt privileged to be invited into this world so different and separate from his own. Taking off his hat, he followed Hira.

Later, after Baines had finished shaking hands and pressing noses as was the warm custom with the Maori people, Hira took his arm. Baines placed his hat on her head affectionately. Then, slipping his hand into one of his deep pockets, he brought forth a tin of tobacco and offered it to Hira. She smiled.

"Peini, I'll miss you," Hira said, "you are human like us." She sighed mournfully. "The *pakeha*, they have no heart, they think only of their land." As she spoke a soft rain began to fall; Baines felt it whisper across his face. A shiver ran through him, almost a premonition, but he shook the feeling away. Accompanied by Hira, he made his way past the meeting house and the low sleeping houses to the *Pa* entrance where his horse stood, tethered and patient.

"Today our enemies are selling their land for guns. Now we too must buy guns. We must sell our land to fight for our land." She shook her head at the injustice wrought against her people.

Baines nodded at Hira. He knew what she said was true, he had no disagreement with her. He mounted his heavily laden horse, and a group gathered to say farewell. Mana, the young man who had been working with Alisdair Stewart earlier that day, pushed forward to say goodbye, but could not get near to where Baines sat, high on his beast. Baines glanced at Mana, and saw the piano key that he had fashioned into an earring dangling from his ear, the white ivory gleaming against his black hair.

Baines rode through the group, which parted messily, surprised at the sudden movement of his horse. Reaching the young man, he took the piano key in his hand, but Mana pulled away.

"It is mine," Mana said defensively. "I found it."

Baines took hold of the earring again and, leaning down low from his mount, gently freed it from Mana's ear. He turned the key over and found the writing. *"Homai ki au—"* he spoke with great urgency, "I want this." He knew that, like himself, none of the Maoris were able to read.

"It's mine," Mana shouted, cross with Baines. "I found it."

"What do you want?" asked Baines. "Ask for it. *Tupeka?*"

Others in the small group began to shout, "Ask for his belt," "his boots," "his gun," and soon the children joined in, reeling off a list of Baines' visible possessions, while Baines himself broke into an agitated grin.

Hatless and gunless, a piece of flax holding up his trousers, Baines rode away from the walls of the *Pa.* It was raining hard now, and George clutched Ada's engraved key to his breast. He rubbed the lettering with the tip of his thumb, pressing the etched letters into his skin as though he might be able to absorb their meaning this way. He rode directly to the one-room school at the far side of the settlement. As he reached the pony paddock, the rain began to ease.

Baines could hear a chorus of tiny voices reciting their times tables and as he peeped through a hole in the wall he saw rows of little legs swinging under wooden tables.

A few moments later, the door flew open and the children straggled down the steps. The girls wore long, stained pinafores and all the children's boots seemed too large for their feet, except for one small boy whose boots were cut open allowing his grubby toes to stick out. Baines stood watching four little girls play a sedate game of skip-rope, using a bush vine, and wondered whom he might approach. Just then a little girl clutching a large book wandered off on her own and sat down beside the crooked stream that ran next to the schoolhouse. Baines sat down beside her. The babbling water passed near their feet.

"Can you read?" he asked.

The little girl, her hair in stiff plaits, closed the book, got up, and walked away without speaking. Baines stood and watched as the child kept walking; she stopped at a safe distance and turned to look at him. Another child, even more petite than the first, dropped down from where she had been perched in a tree. "I can," she said, her voice clear and piping.

"You can read?" he said doubtfully. The child seemed very small.

"Yes . . . lots of things." The other girls abandoned their skipping and gathered around the tiny child.

"She can't read," a bigger girl said disdainfully, "she's my sister. I ought to know." She eyed the open jar that Baines held in one hand. "Are those sweets?"

"I can read!" the littlest girl said indignantly.

"She can't," contradicted her big sister. Baines held out the sweets jar to the small child. "Don't give her one." Baines allowed the girl to take a sweet anyway. "She can't read," the older girl insisted.

The smaller girl popped the sweet into her pretty mouth and threw the wrapper away; one of the others immediately picked it up and held it to her nose, eager for the scent. "Mmm, caramels," she said, handing the wrapper to the other children.

"Can you read?" Baines asked the older girl, his impatience beginning to surface. He held forth the piano key.

The girl took it from his hand with great authority. Her friends crowded behind her, all vying for a better view. She frowned at the writing, turning the key over to look at the other side. "Running writing," she commented, "we haven't done that yet."

"Myrtle can read it," volunteered another child, "her mother taught her."

The key was snatched from the bigger girl and given to Myrtle, the girl with the book whom Baines had first approached. Everyone watched, rapt as Myrtle struggled to read the inscription.

"D e a r   G e o r g e . . ." She frowned. The children all looked at Baines to see if this was right so far. He nodded encouragingly. "Y o u . . ." one or two children joined Myrtle in reading these words, ". . . have . . ." "That's 'my,' " the big sister interrupted.

"It's not an 'M.' "

"Yes it is."

Together the two girls reiterated. "Dear—George—you—have—my—" They paused.

"—heart?" suggested Myrtle uncertainly. She pulled a face as if confused, then read on: "Ada McGrath."

"It doesn't make sense," said the big girl.

The little girls all read the message together again. Myrtle turned the key over matter of factly as if expecting to see more writing. "That's all . . ." she said, looking up at Baines.

"Say it again, just you," said Baines.

Everyone turned to listen to Myrtle. "Dear George, you have my heart, Ada McGrath." She gave a little shrug.

"You say it," Baines pointed to the older girl.

"Dear George," she spoke slowly, her voice deep, "you have my heart, Ada McGrath."

Another little girl spontaneously recited the message. As did another. And another. Through all this Baines kept his head down, shaking it in disbelief and shy happiness. He started to laugh, with relief and delight. The girls began to laugh as well, thinking that the message must be a joke. They continued to repeat it, and each rephrasing appeared to give Baines fresh pleasure. Meanwhile, the smallest of the girls quietly helped herself to the sweets.

At Stewart's house, Alisdair Stewart, Aunt Morag, and Nessie struggled to carry Ada, unconscious, her clothes heavy with mud and blood, through the whitestumped marsh in the rain.

Inside, the two women removed Ada's clothes, cutting through her sleeves with scissors, their own faces and dresses now smeared with muck. Both women were very distressed. "Oh dear," said Morag, "what an accident." As she peeled back the cloth, Ada's arm seemed too frail and thin, the sight of her pale blue skin almost as upsetting. "And she had wood enough already . . . If she doesn't die of blood loss, we will lose her to pneumonia. HOT WATER!" she demanded. "The mud is everywhere," Morag muttered darkly.

"Oh, the poor wee thing . . ." said Nessie, whose own eyes brimmed with tears of sympathy, ". . . ohhh dear . . . ."

Stewart entered the bedroom bearing hot water. He was subdued, anxious, looking on hopelessly, unable to be of much use. "Now off you go," said Morag, pushing him out, "that glum staring will cure no one."

Stewart left then, closing the door. He had told his aunt that Ada had slipped while chopping wood, that he had been working elsewhere and had found her in the mud, and he had run for their help without thinking. The lie formed a hard nut in his throat; he could not swallow. He could not swallow any of it.

Morag continued to clean Ada's wounded hand while Nessie tore sheets into bandage-width strips. Ada was now semiconscious, her eyelids fluttering and closing, while her lips moved, as if to speak.

"Look at these lips . . ." Morag said suddenly. "What a story they try to tell."

Nessie began to comb Ada's hair with great care and tenderness, stroking her like she would a child. Ada shivered. "Might I put a blanket on?" suggested Nessie to Morag. "She is quite cooled down."

"Yes, very well, very well."

Nessie pulled the cover over Ada. The two older women looked at her lying there, at her white, anguished face skewered with pain. Nessie reached out to stroke her black hair again. "Ohh so soft. Soft."

"One of God's difficult daughters," said Morag. "Yet, one can feel *Him* in her, frightening like a storm."

*A*s DUSK fell, George rode to his hut, silly with happiness. He repeated Ada's message of love to himself over and over, the words becoming a sweet ballad. His was smiling as his horse cantered up the slope; then he saw Hira, running toward him, her face contorted as she shouted, "Peini, Peini, the little girl, I saw her come up here, screaming . . ."

George swung down from his saddle and started to run. "Blood on her. Looked bad . . ." Hira said, "very bad . . ." The door of his hut was open. George went quickly up the steps, followed by Hira.

Inside Flora crouched in a corner. Her face was chalky, tear-stained, and splattered with mud, she was soaked to the bone. Her angel wings were squashed behind her and blood was clearly visible, smeared across the front of her pinafore. As George came through the door, she began to cry loudly with relief.

George rushed to where she was huddled against the

wall. "What has happened?" He stroked her hair away from her face. "Hush, hush. What is it?"

Flora handed him her grim parcel. George took the blood-soaked package and unwrapped it, revealing Ada's tiny severed finger.

"You're not to see her or he'll chop her up!" cried Flora, sobbing and shutting her eyes against what the package contained.

"What happened?" said George fiercely, taking her by the shoulders. Flora struggled, and George's grip tightened. She began to scream and, breaking free, she ran outside. "Tell me!" George shouted, chasing her. He caught her and shook her roughly, demanding, "Where is she?" He lifted the girl who now shrieked, high, jagged cries, unable to stop. "Shh!" he shook her again. "Quiet down! Where is she?" he shouted.

"He chopped it off," Flora screamed, sobbing.

"What did she tell him?" cried George. "What did she tell him?" But Hira came and lifted the child from George's grasp. "She's just a little girl," she said, holding the child gently, soothing her, smoothing her wet hair from her terrified face.

"I want to crush his skull," George said, his voice full of rancor and bitter despair, and Flora began to scream again. "No, no, he'll chop it off."

George Baines beat his fists against the trunk of a tree, moaning with frustration and impotent rage.

$\mathcal{T}$HAT night the bush stirred quietly, the cicadas and night creatures keeping a low chorus. Alisdair Stewart entered Ada McGrath's bedroom carrying a lamp. He put it down on her bedside table. He studied her pale face, beaded with perspiration, her hair glued to her cheeks and neck, her lips cracked and dry. She slept. He spoke softly, as though she were awake and listening.

"You pushed me too hard," he said quietly. "You can not send love to him, you can not do that." He shook his finger at her. "Even to think about it makes me very angry." He searched for words, straining for control. "I meant to love you," Alisdair Stewart told his sleeping wife. "I clipped your wings, that is all."

Stewart leaned over and began to stroke Ada's forehead and cheek. He sang softly, the words of a love ballad welled up from somewhere in his memory: "We will be together, you will see it will be better . . ." Ada stirred in her sleep, brushing his hand away from her face. Her forehead was damp with fever; she thrashed under the covers.

"Are you hot?" asked Stewart, ". . . my sweet love bird." He pulled the covers down to cool her. Her nightdress was sodden with sweat and clung to her body, her right hand now bandaged, rested on her stomach. As he pulled down the sheets and tried to make her more comfortable, Stewart saw that the top of her leg, the soft, creamy inside of her upper thigh, was exposed. Lifting her leg slightly and slipping one hand beneath it, Stewart began to stroke her skin. A feeling of pleasure grew and built as his hand lingered. He bent to lower his face to her skin, pressing his lips against her, burying his face between her legs, inhaling deeply.

Ada stirred in her sleep again. Stewart looked at her face, his hand edging higher under her nightdress. A new thought occurred to him, a terrible thought that he attempted to spurn, but as he had phrased the thought to himself, he could not resist it. He glanced at her face, still fevered and unconscious. Stealthily, he began to undo his belt buckle, then he bent across his wife to gently separate her legs. As he moved his body over her, intent on his task, he looked toward her face again and, to his shame and horror, saw that she was looking directly back at him, her eyes perfectly focused on his. Without speaking, his breath quick and labored, Stewart stopped what he was doing and moved away, gently pulling down her gown.

"Feeling better?" he asked guilefully.

Ada's lips moved slightly. Suddenly sure he had heard something, Stewart looked at Ada intently, lowering himself closer to her lips, his eyes locked on hers. "What . . .?" The sound of his own voice made him blink. He watched her as if listening to her speak in a voice so faint and distant that it required great concentration and perseverance to hear it. As he watched her, his face transformed; his eyes filled, his lips softened, and his eyebrows took on the exact expression of Ada's own.

The kerosene lamp burned fitfully, fluttering a light pulse across their faces. Stewart moved closer to Ada.

Outside the wind banged the roof and rubbed branches against each other, making a high-pitched seesaw sound. He leaned closer still, listening.

Rising, Stewart put on his coat and, taking a lamp and a gun, made his way through the ghostly tree stumps and the dark bush beyond to the hut of George Baines. He stepped over the curled, sleeping figure of Hira on the veranda and into the hut, where a fire still burned. Over the hearth hung Flora's clothes, washed and dripping. He approached the bed and saw Flora wrapped in a blanket with Baines beside her, axe in hand, both fast asleep. Stewart nudged Baines awake with the butt of his rifle, prodding him under the chin. Baines woke with a start, and was frozen by the sight of Stewart with his gun.

Stewart stared at his foe, examining him in the flickering firelight. "Put that away," he said, indicating the axe, "on the floor." He spoke quietly and slowly, his expression veering from madness to lucidity. Baines obeyed.

Slowly Stewart began to speak. "I look at you, at your face. I have had that face in my head, hating it. But now I am here seeing it . . . It is nothing." Stewart moved the gun from Baines' chin to his temple. "You have your marks, you look at me through your eyes, yes, you are even afraid of me." Stewart laughed, and it was chilling. "Look at you!" he said. "Get up."

Baines sat up, careful not to disturb Flora who slept on. He felt calm. The piano key, with its glorious message, lay safe under his pillow.

"Has Ada ever spoken to you?"

"You mean in signs?"

Stewart shook his head. "No, words. Have you ever heard words?"

Baines looked suspicious. "No, not words."

"You never thought you heard words?"

Baines shook his head.

Stewart lifted one hand to his forehead. "She has spoken to me. I heard it here." He pressed his palm against his brow, his eyes wide. "I heard her voice here in my head. I watched her lips, they did not make the words. Yet . . . the harder I listened, the clearer I heard her, as clear as I hear my own voice."

"Spoken words?" asked Baines.

"No, but her words are in my head." Stewart paused. "I know what you think, that it's a trick, that I am making it up. No, the words I heard were her words."

"What were they?" He did not know if it was Stewart's pain or his madness speaking but either way Baines listened. In Stewart he saw someone he never expected; in this wide-eyed stiff man he saw himself, helpless, hopeless, love-lost, and for that instant Baines loved him.

Stewart looked up at the ceiling as if reciting something he had learned by heart and meant to repeat exactly: "She said, 'I am afraid of my will, of what it might do, it is so strange and strong.' She said," Stewart hesitated, then nodded his head, " 'I have to go. Let me go. Let Baines take me away.' "

"You punished her wrongly," Baines interrupted angrily. "It was me, my fault."

Stewart did not reply.

Flora stirred in her sleep, sighing. Her brow frowned, then smoothed, her eyelids fluttering as her eyes darted back and forth, dreaming.

Then Stewart, his eyes full of tears, continued: "Understand me, I am here for her, for her . . . I wonder that I don't wake, that I am not asleep to be here talking with you. I love her. But what is the use? She doesn't care for me. I wish her gone. I wish you gone. I want to wake and find that this is all a dream, that's what I want." Stewart nodded as though confirming what he had just said. "I want to believe I am not this man. I want myself back; the one I knew."

𝒜 D A lay awake. She knew Alisdair Stewart had gone to George Baines. She had lost much blood, and in her weakened state knew there was nothing she could do. She wondered, presently, if Stewart would kill George, and this thought sent a shudder through her soul.

Chapter *11*

$\mathcal{I}$N her father's house, Ada McGrath had known almost immediately that she was with child, an instinctive recognition of the signs without having ever been told what they might be. She had passed into puberty without a mother's explanation, only a stern housemaid to ease her concern that she might bleed to death. She knew now, with calm certainty, what the signs portended.

After that night in the piano room, Delwar Haussler had fled the McGrath house. When Ada had left him, kissing him good-night in the music room early Christmas morning, he had gone to his own room to pace the floor until he heard the household stirring. He waited until he heard the voice of Wyston McGrath in the kitchen below, issuing orders and making recommendations for the lunch menu. Then he put on the frock coat and velvet cap in which he had arrived nearly two years previously, and went down the stairs. In one hand he held a carefully penned resignation notice.

"What's this?" boomed Wyston, on receiving Delwar in his office, fingering the piece of paper which Delwar had sealed with wax.

"Open it, sir," said Delwar, "you will find my notice to quit."

Wyston frowned. He thought only of little Ada. Her heart might break at the cessation of her lessons.

"Are you unhappy here?"

"I wish to return to my family . . ." Delwar searched for words, for excuses. "I should like to marry." He gasped at his falsehood, amazed at his own temerity. He knew marriage to Ada was out of the question and felt at that moment as though he would never consider the possibility again.

"Oh," Wyston blustered. He embarrassed so easily. "Well, in that case . . . When do you intend to leave?"

"I shall go today, sir."

"Oh," said Ada's father, again searching for words. Then he remembered. "But it is Christmas Day. There are no carriages, no services of any kind."

"I shall walk for a while, sir."

"On the Lord's birthday? With the possibility of snow?" Wyston thought the man mad.

"Yes."

"Very well." The young man's foolhardiness was not his concern. "You have been of good service. Wait, and I shall draft your renumeration." Wyston decided that it was best to let him go; if the boy was mad he was better off somewhere else. "Perhaps you would like to say good-bye to Ada. I'll have the maid wake her." He raised his arm to ring his service bell.

"No, sir," Delwar said quickly, reaching out to stay McGrath's hand. "I'm sure she is still sleeping and I would not like to disturb her with this news."

"So I shall have to be the one to tell her, eh? Hmm. You've got this very well worked out."

Delwar blushed at the old man's accusation. "I will go and gather my things. I shall send for my possessions at the nearest convenience."

"Very well," said Wyston gruffly. "Very well. I will leave the bank draft on the entrance table."

"Thank you, sir," Delwar said, backing out of the room. "Your daughter is possessed of a fine talent."

"A dark talent," muttered Wyston, "that is what I say."

But young Ada was not asleep, she had been unable to rest after returning to her room, suffused with the dual excitements of the pleasures of Christmas Day and Delwar Haussler's embrace. She too had paced her room, hugging her body, thinking of what had passed that evening. In the morning she had dressed quickly and gone down to the kitchen, where she had been informed that her father was in his office. She stepped lightly along the corridor, her high spirits matched by the blaze of health in her cheeks. She held her narrow shoulders straight, her spine in a perfect line.

Ada stopped short of her father's door when she heard

voices inside. A strange premonition passed through her; she slipped behind the door to listen instead of entering the room with Christmas cheer as she had intended. From her hiding place she heard every word of Delwar Haussler's leave-taking. Just as she had willed herself not to speak at the age of six, she now willed herself not to cry out, not to interrupt this terrible conversation. She stood still as stone in the hallway, scarcely breathing, her heart slowing within her small, stiff frame. She remained behind the door while Delwar Haussler went up to his room and gathered his things. She stayed motionless as a statue while her father came out of his office, depositing the piano tutor's wages on the entrance table. She did not move until after Delwar Haussler had come down the stairs, picked up the envelope, opened the front door, and departed.

$\mathcal{H}$ E R pregnancy progressed as such things do, her size in direct disproportion to her height and normal weight. It was the housemaid who did her washing who first passed comment, noticing that certain seams had been stretched to bursting, then realizing that Ada McGrath had not bled regularly of late. The staff discussed it for days in the kitchen and the garden, although if Ada was aware of this she did not betray it. Her heart had broken, but she did not betray that either. She continued to spend her afternoons in the music room. For a time she had played the duets on her own because it suited her mood, but she grew tired of this lopsided harmony. She began to return to her old methods of music-making, the improvisations she had once let lead her through the afternoons, her playing now vastly enriched, however, by her months and months of tutoring.

It was the senior maid who took it upon herself to speak to the master about his daughter's condition. No one dared to speak to Ada herself; the girl had become even more forbidding and aloof than she had seemed previously. "What?" Wyston had shouted, his voice reverberating through the household. Ada was upstairs playing the piano. She paused between phrases, knowing he had been told, then she continued to pursue her melody.

Wyston had been too embarrassed by this revelation to approach his daughter; he left that to Beadsley, the lawyer. Beadsley had met with Ada intending a stern lecture and reproach, thinking that she could be persuaded to reveal the identity of the father so that something could be done, a marriage arranged, at the very least reparations made. But, of course, Ada would reveal nothing. She refused to write a single word, pushing the sheet of paper away each time Beadsley offered it her. Finally exasperated, Beadsley left the room and gone back to McGrath, announcing that there was nothing to be done. The girl would maintain her silence on the matter, she was not to be traversed. The men decided that Ada would remain housebound for the duration of her confinement. No one would be told. Everyone would know anyway. No further effort would be made to discover the identity of the father. Perhaps, offered Beadsley hopefully, the dishonorable fellow would come forth eventually.

After that, Wyston McGrath remained strangely silent on the topic. He watched his daughter grow large and larger still. Some of the staff maintained that there were times when he confused his daughter with his dead wife, slipping back through the years to when Cecilia had carried Ada. Others in the town insinuated with shameful whispers that perhaps it was Wyston himself who had fathered the child. But most knew who the father must have been, and talk of his sudden departure slithered through the streets of Aberdeen. Some were scandalized by McGrath's seeming lack of indignation; why was the young man not searched out, made to take responsibility? Others said that McGrath was too grand to admit his daughter might form a liaison with a mere musician, a piano tutor, and only a minor talent at that.

But the McGraths themselves maintained a silence as broad as it was deep. Wyston treated his daughter with increasing tenderness; he stopped thinking about her unmarried state, and from time to time entertained the notion that perhaps she had willed herself into bearing a child, her will was that strong. When the time came, he retreated into his office and paced the floor all the long night. Ada was tortured by the duration of her labor; it was thought that perhaps her pelvis was too narrow for the birth to be straightforward. However, with the arrival of the surgeon, the child's passage into life came quickly.

The news of Flora's birth was taken to Wyston immediately—a girl, oh how it brought Cecilia back to him. He was frightened that his daughter might now meet the same fate as his wife, but the surgeon, an old friend, assured him of Ada's sturdy constitution.

And although Wyston himself had no trouble accepting his only grandchild into his heart, the town of Aberdeen was less benevolent, and Ada was forced into a life of enclosure, rarely leaving the estate. After a few initial visits with the child to church had been greeted by loud whispers and crass stares, Wyston was told by the serving minister that the child could not be baptized, and so the McGraths severed their formal ties with the church. This caused Wyston great pain as a man of conventional faith, but it did not trouble Ada. The child was absorbing, beauty itself with her tiny hands and feet. She would lie in her basket under the piano while Ada played, one foot on the pedals, the other rocking the child.

Ada took much pleasure in watching her child grow. She felt no lack in her life, herself restored to full health rapidly. At night she sometimes had trouble sleeping, not connected to the baby's wakefulness. At these times she thought of Delwar Haussler, remembering his embrace. He had been a coward, that had been revealed by his departure. Ada wondered then if all men were cowardly when pushed. She did not care that he had not asked to marry her, she was no longer concerned that he had not written to her, or even left a note explaining why he had gone. But she did long to listen to him, to sit beside him while he played the piano, once again.

$\mathcal{T}$HE years passed and Flora grew, and Ada too grew into adulthood. Wyston stalled again and again on the long overdue visit from his sisters Patricia and Ethel, Ada's maiden aunts, as he was unable to countenance their questions and the inevitability of their judgment, which he feared would be harsh. The town continued to talk, as towns do, speculation fueled by lack of information, like a fire ravenous for oxygen. Once, when Flora was seven and the pair ventured into town in search of a birthday present for Wyston, a local woman greeted their presence with a self-righteous hurrah, and spat with Christian piety on the cobbles of the street before them.

Hearing of this, Wyston conceived the idea of advertising in the colonial press for a husband for his daughter and her child. And it was this notice that came to the attention of Alisdair Stewart, thousands and thousands of miles away in New Zealand, Britain's tropical mirror, sending Ada McGrath on her long journey to meet him.

$\mathcal{A}$DA emerged from Alisdair Stewart's house into the new morning as though somnambulant once again, dressed for leave-taking. She could not absorb all that had passed since her arrival. The Maori men were busy shifting her trunks and suitcases. Aunt Morag and Nessie stood in the doorway watching, shocked and saddened by the terrible events, Morag muttering, "Oh dear, oh dear," under her breath. In their hearts, they were glad to see the woman leave. Alisdair would not be the same. She had damaged him in some way, of that they were certain.

Ada was unconcerned by the thoughts of Aunt Morag and Nessie, she had sustained damage enough of her own. She stepped out of the doorway cautiously, blinking and squinting, as though she had not seen the light of day for weeks. Flora stood with George; they were both neatly dressed, Flora's blue bonnet tied around her chin, George in his blue frock coat. George kept a protective arm around Flora, and the child clung to the man's trousers, shivering at the sight of her mother's arm in its sling. Alisdair Stewart was nowhere to be seen. Ada wore black as though in mourning and her hair was loose under her bonnet, she could not plait it, nor did she care. The Maori men talked amongst themselves, stealing glances at Ada, but the *pakeha* did not speak.

The sun streamed through the high branches of the *kauri* trees as the long trek back to the beach began. George took Ada to one side. Without speaking, he looked urgently into her dark, bruised eyes. He removed his hat and moved closer to her, kissing her on the mouth with enormous passion and tenderness, in full view of the company, as if in confirmation of all that had passed. Ada received the kiss but felt nothing. The brutality of the

past days had numbed her. She was dazed and humiliated.

On the beach, the same beach where they had arrived
barely three months previously, Ada sat on a trunk while
Flora gently tried to neaten her hair, hoping that if it
were made good she too would be better again. George
had arranged with the Maoris for their goods, and themselves, to be transported away from the settlement. At the
water's edge an enormous and ornately carved seagoing
Maori canoe was being loaded with their trunks, the
piano last of all. Flora carefully placed Ada's bonnet on
her head.

Flora and Ada were lifted into the canoe, which still
rested on the sand, the piano balanced precariously.
George helped with the rigging of the instrument; thick
rope ends coiled under the women's feet.

"*Tarmaharawa—aianei tahuri ai*—It's too heavy—the
canoe will capsize," said the oarsman Kamira.

"*Keite pai! Kaare e titahataha ana*—The piano is all right.
It's balanced," replied George Baines.

"*Peini*, only a madman would take it."

"She needs it, she must have it," George replied.

Finally, they were ready. Chanting rhythmically, the
men pushed the boat out toward the sea, six men on each
side of the burdened canoe, leaving a heavy groove in the
sand where they passed. George's friend Hira stood alone
on the beach. Tears ran openly down her sad face as she
sang her farewell to Peini.

He rimu teretere koe ete. Peini eeeii,
Tere Ki Tawhiti Ki Pamamao eeeii
He waka Teretere He waka teretere.
Ko koe ka tere ki tua whakarere eeeii.

You are like seaweed drifting in the sea, Baines,
Drift far away, drift far beyond the horizon.
A canoe glides hither, a canoe glides thither,
But you though will journey on and eventually
be beyond the veil.

Once seaborne, the Maoris continued their chant as they paddled vigorously through the choppy waves. The heavy canoe sat very low in the water, a small fleck on the great breadth of the sea. Flora thought she might be sick, but she stared out toward the horizon instead. George took Ada's good hand in his, gently. He knew she was not well, but he trusted that with rest and her piano beside her she would gradually recover.

After a while, Ada's eyes turned the color of steel. She removed her hand from George's and signed to Flora, who looked at her mother, then at Baines, amazed.

"What did she say?" asked George.

"She says, 'Throw the piano overboard.' "

"It's quite safe, they are managing." George thought Ada needed reassuring. Ada signed again, more vehemently.

"She doesn't want it," said Flora firmly. "She says it's spoiled."

"I have the key, I'll have it mended," said George, pulling the carved block of wood and ivory from his breast pocket. Ada shook her head, miming directly to George, her determination increasing.

Kamira, the oarsman, overheard. He turned to speak, "Yes, she's right, push it over, it's a coffin."

"Please, Ada," said George. Ada began to rise, he pulled her back down again, "Ada! You will regret it. It's your piano, I want you to have it."

"She doesn't want it," Flora insisted as Ada stood, pulling at the ropes. "Throw it over!"

"Sit down!" George said sharply. "All right. We'll throw it over."

The piano was broken, she was broken, it could never be as it was. She wanted the piano gone.

As the men began to untie the guy ropes, maneuvering the piano to the edge, Ada looked down into the turquoise, translucent water, trailing her hand, wondering what lay beneath the surface. She watched as the men rapidly lifted the planks on which the piano balanced. In an instant, the piano slid into the sea. It made a great splash, and the canoe rocked violently. The loose ropes sped their way after it. Ada watched them snake past her feet and then, out of that fatal curiosity that had always been her way, odd and undisciplined, she placed her foot among the loops. Should she not share the same fate as the piano? Were she and her piano not one?

The rope tightened and gripped her ankle so that she was suddenly snatched from the boat into the sea and pulled by the piano down through the cold water.

Bubbles tumbled from her mouth. Down she fell, down and down, her eyes open, her clothes twisting about her. The Maoris diving after her could not reach her as she plunged on into the depths. Long moments passed. Ada looked around at the darkness of the ocean. There is no sound under water, Ada thought, as she plummeted further into the fathomless sea: silence affects everyone in the end. She looked up, at her bandaged and damaged right hand, at the light as it faded from above her, the bottom of the canoe almost gone from sight, at the darkness all around. She felt a great stillness.

She made her choice.

Ada began to struggle. She kicked at the rope, but it held tight around her foot, the enormous weight of the piano pulling the line taut. She reached down to it and kicked hard again. Then, using her other foot, she levered herself free of her boot. The piano and her empty boot continued their eerie, soundless fall, while, suddenly released, light and free, Ada's body willed itself to the surface. Filling her lungs with air, she was met and brought to safety by the Maori divers and lifted into the canoe, into the sunshine, by George Baines.

What a death!
What a chance!
What a surprise!
My will has chosen life!
Still, it has had me spooked, and many others besides.

Epilogue

𝓜USLIN curtains billowed in the soft breeze as Ada paced the balcony, her head covered by a dark cloth. She was practicing the consonants, strange to her throat and lips, her sound still so bad she was ashamed. She taught piano now, in Nelson. George had fashioned her a metal fingertip and, with it, she was quite the town freak, which satisfied.

George had bought a fine house with the remainder of his whaling money—money that came from the living ocean, like Ada herself had done that day. He established himself with a trading business from the port; he made good use of his old contacts, both Maori and whaler. Flora began school, clattering in her new shoes from England on the first day. Together, the three lived like survivors, fragile and fearful at first, then slowly, as time passed, they began to like their new life and marveled at the grace that had delivered them.

At night I think of my piano in its ocean grave, and sometimes of myself floating above it. Down there everything is so still and silent that it lulls me to sleep. It is a weird lullaby and so it is; it is mine.

There is a silence where hath been no sound

There is a silence where no sound may be,

In the cold grave—under the deep, deep sea . . .

THOMAS HOOD (1799–1845)

Acknowledgments

$\mathscr{I}$T is with gratitude that I acknowledge four women who made this novel possible: Sue Berger who initially inspired me to write two chapters; Kate Pullinger, a novelist in her own right who wrote and rearranged the text; Lesley Bryce, who edited it; and Francesca Gonshaw whose vision and enthusiasm held us all together and had me contributing far more than I had ever planned to.

I'd also like to thank Colin Englert, Liz Calder, Viccy Harper, Bob and Harvey Weinstein, Scott Greenstein, and the staff at Miramax and Hyperion.

Jane Campion, March 1994